WORDPERFECT 6 FOR WINDOWS:

THE POCKET REFERENCE

Patricia Shepard and
Carole Boggs Matthews

Osborne **McGraw-Hill**

Berkeley New York St. Louis San Francisco
Auckland Bogotá Hamburg London Madrid
Mexico City Milan Montreal New Delhi Panama City
Paris São Paulo Singapore Sydney
Tokyo Toronto

Osborne **McGraw-Hill**
2600 Tenth Street
Berkeley, California 94710
U.S.A.

For information on translations or book distributors outside of the U.S.A., please write to Osborne **McGraw-Hill** at the above address.

WordPerfect 6 for Windows: The Pocket Reference

34567890 DOC 9987654

ISBN 0-07-882003-0

CONTENTS

Appendix

Introduction

The Pocket Reference provides a quick source of information about the various commands, functions, and features in WordPerfect 6.0 for Windows. This book can be used by either beginners or more experienced users. It is especially helpful when you are using a feature with which you are familiar but need to be reminded of the specific keystrokes, menus, or mouse actions that are required to produce the results you want. For those who are new to WordPerfect, general information about starting WordPerfect and about producing documents is also included.

The book contains two main sections plus an appendix that lists the shortcut keys and the features to which they have been assigned.

The "Basic" section discusses features that are common to most word processing programs, such as creating, editing, saving, and printing; moving around in a document; and formatting. In addition, the components of the WordPerfect window are identified, as well as the menu bar categories and the cascading menu for each. Also included here is a discussion of how to work with multiple windows and how to move from WordPerfect for Windows to other Windows applications. This section is especially helpful for those users who are just beginning to use WordPerfect 6.0 for Windows.

The "Features and Commands" section presents each feature, function, or command in alphabetical order so that you can get to it quickly. Numbered steps are presented for each item, as well as a brief description of what it does and any other information that is especially relevant to the feature. Ideas for using the feature will be given for some items, where it is appropriate. Also included, in some cases, are lists of options that are available when the feature is being used.

The "Appendix" contains an alphabetical list of functions and commands and the shortcut keys that are assigned to execute each.

Conventions used in this pocket reference:

- **Boldface** is used to indicate either keys to be pressed, options to be chosen, or text to be typed.
- *Italic* is used to call attention to specific features or terms.
- Underlined characters in menu options are hot keys that can be pressed to choose that item or option.
- A plus sign between keys indicates that they are to pressed together—that is, the first key is held down, press the next key, and then release them. When three keys are combined, press them in the order given and then release the keys.
- Numbered steps without a heading are steps that can be performed using either the keyboard or the mouse. When keyboard and mouse actions are different for a specific feature, headings are displayed identifying the steps for each. Shortcut keys, when they are assigned to a feature, will be shown in parentheses, such as CTRL+ENTER.

Basics

This section covers the basics: how to start and exit WordPerfect for Windows, what the screen and menu structure are like, and basic word processing functions such as creating, editing, saving, opening, and printing documents. Also included are instructions for choosing options using the mouse and the keyboard, moving around in the document, working with multiple documents, and moving from WordPerfect to other applications.

Starting WordPerfect for Windows

The procedure for starting WordPerfect for Windows is similar to starting other Windows applications. The installation process automatically creates an icon for WordPerfect, as well as for the Speller, Thesaurus, QuickFinder, Kickoff, and the installation program. These icons are in the WPWin 6.0 group. To start WordPerfect for Windows:

1. Turn on the computer and start Windows.
2. Double-click on the WPWin 6.0 group icon. (If the group icon is already open, skip this step.)
3. Double-click on the WPWin 6.0 program icon.

Note *If you are using the keyboard rather than a mouse, press* CTRL+TAB *to select the WPWin 6.0 group icon and press* ENTER *to open it. Then in the group window press any of the arrow keys to select the WPWin 6.0 icon and press* ENTER *to start the application.*

The screen will show a new blank document window.

Window Information

The first time you start WordPerfect, the window resembles the one shown here. You can change the window display, either for the current word processing session or permanently. Refer to PREFERENCES in "Features and Commands" for instructions on making permanent changes.

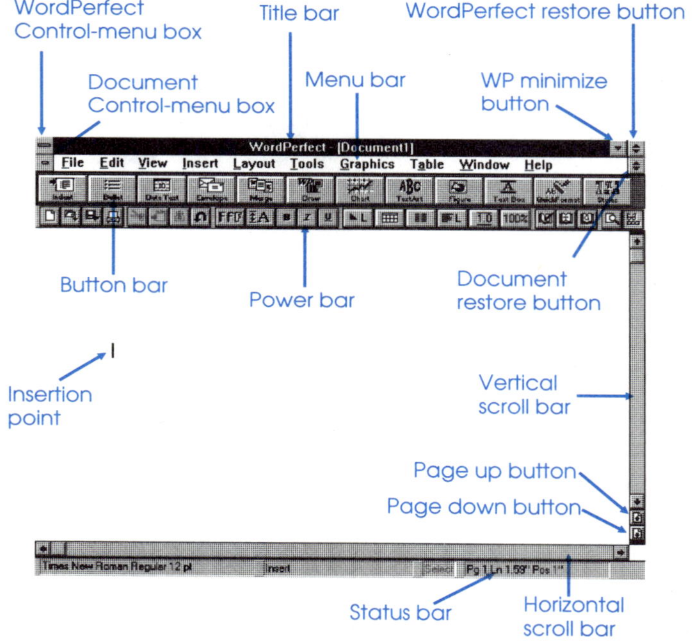

The features shown here and their uses are

- *WordPerfect Control-menu box* Moves, sizes, or closes the application window, or switches to another application window. A maximized window cannot be moved or sized.
- *Document Control-menu box* Moves, sizes, or closes a document window, or goes to the next document

window. A maximized window cannot be moved or sized.

- *Insertion point* Indicates the position in the document where you are working.
- *Title bar* Displays the name of the application and the name of the document.
- *WordPerfect minimize button* Reduces the WordPerfect window to an icon. Double-click on the icon to redisplay the WordPerfect window.
- *WordPerfect restore button* Changes the WordPerfect window to a medium-sized window in the Program Manager.
- *Document restore button* Changes the document window to a medium-sized window in the WordPerfect window.
- *Menu bar* Shows the main categories for each group of menu items. As you drag across the menu bar or drag down through a cascading menu, a brief description of each item is displayed in the title bar.
- *Button bar* Contains buttons that insert some WordPerfect features such as date text, figures, text art, and charts; or that quickly format text with indents, bullets, or styles. Envelope and merge buttons are also included in the Button Bar so that you can access those features. When you point to a button, its name, a description of its usage, and the shortcut key for it are displayed in the title bar. Refer to BUTTON BAR in "Features and Commands" for instructions for moving the bar to a new position.
- *Power bar* Contains buttons that can be used to perform some WordPerfect functions without going to the menu. When you point to a button, its name, a description of its usage, and the shortcut key for it are displayed in the title bar.
- *Vertical scroll bar* Used with the mouse, moves the document up and down or goes from one page to the next. Up and down arrows, page up and page down

buttons, and a shaded box that can be dragged up or down are included in the scroll bar.

- *Horizontal scroll bar* Used with the mouse, moves the document to the left or right in the window. Left and right arrows and a shaded box that can be dragged right or left are included in the scroll bar.
- *Status bar* Displays the current location of the insertion point and the font style that is being used. It displays the word "Select" in bold when text is selected. You can customize the status bar to add other items to it (Preferences). Refer to PREFERENCES in "Features and Commands."

Menu Structure

The menu bar shows the main categories of items that are available for your word processing work. When one of these is chosen, a list of options will be displayed in a cascading menu. Figure 1 shows the menu options or items in each category.

When a menu item is selected, the title bar displays the item name, a description of what it does, and the shortcut keys, if any, that can be used to perform the action.

A menu item followed by an ellipsis (...) will show a dialog box when it is chosen. (Dialog boxes are discussed in the next section.) A menu item followed by a triangle pointer (▶) will show a cascading menu.

Dialog Boxes

Dialog boxes allow you to enter information as you are using commands. An example of the Tab Set dialog box is shown here. The various types of buttons and boxes in a dialog box are described in the following list.

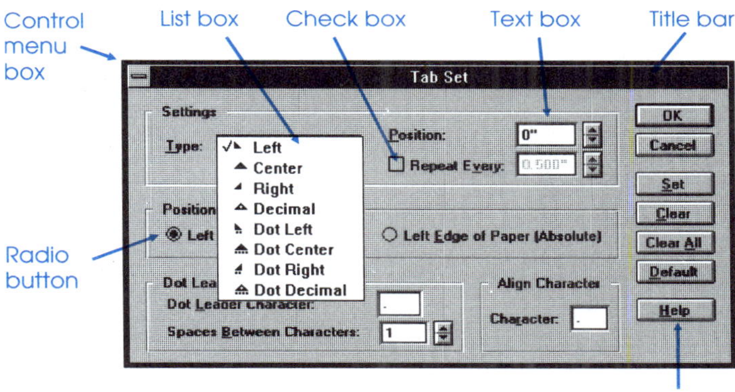

The features in a dialog box and their uses are

- *Control-menu box* Moves or closes the box.
- *Radio buttons* Allow you to select options from a group. Only one choice can be made. A dot appears in the circle when a choice is selected.
- *Check boxes* Allow you to turn an option on or off. An X appears in the box when it is turned on.
- *Title bar* Shows the name of the dialog box.
- *Text box* Allows you to type information, or in some cases when incrementing (arrow) buttons are displayed at the end of a text box, you can select information from a list.
- *Command buttons* Perform specific functions or commands when they are chosen. Some command buttons have ellipses, indicating another dialog box is displayed when the command is selected.
- *List box* Shows a list of choices, or you may have to point to the up or down arrow and hold down the left mouse button to display the list. Then you can drag to the choice you want. If you are using a keyboard, press the UP ARROW or DOWN ARROW to move through the list and highlight the choice you want.

a. File menu

File
New Ctrl+N
Template... Ctrl+T
Open... Ctrl+O
Close Ctrl+F4
Save Ctrl+S
Save As... F3
QuickFinder...
Master Document ▸
Compare Document ▸
Document Summary...
Document Info...
Preferences...
Print... F5
Select Printer...
Mail...
Exit Alt+F4
1 new.wpd

b. Edit menu

Edit
Undo Ctrl+Z
Undelete... Ctrl+Shift+Z
Repeat...
Cut Ctrl+X
Copy Ctrl+C
Paste Ctrl+V
Append
Select ▸
Paste Special...
Links...
Object...
Find... F2
Replace... Ctrl+F2
Go To... Ctrl+G
Convert Case ▸

c. View menu

View
Draft Ctrl+F5
✓Page Alt+F5
Two Page
Zoom...
✓Button Bar
✓Power Bar
Ruler Bar Alt+Shift+F3
✓Status Bar
Hide Bars Alt+Shift+F5
✓Graphics
Table Gridlines
Hidden Text
Show ¶ Ctrl+Shift+F3
Reveal Codes Alt+F3

d. Insert menu

Insert
Bullets & Numbers...
Character... Ctrl+W
Abbreviations...
Date ▸
Other ▸
Footnote ▸
Endnote ▸
Comment ▸
Sound...
Bookmark...
Spreadsheet/Database ▸
File...
Object...
Page Break Ctrl+Enter

e. Layout menu

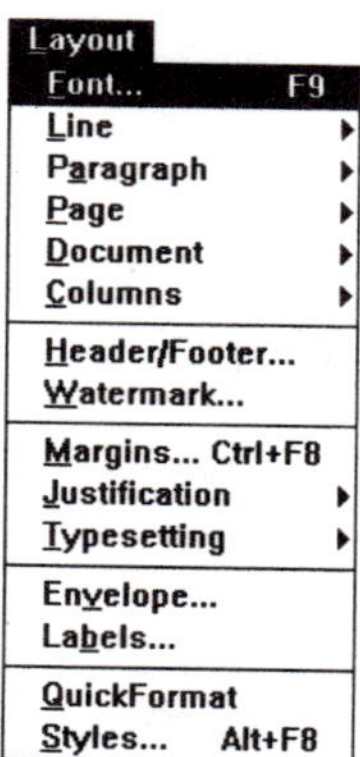

Figure 1 WordPerfect for Windows menu structure

Tools menu

f.

Tools
Speller... Ctrl+F1
Thesaurus... Alt+F1
Grammatik... Alt+Shift+F1
Language...
Macro
Merge... Shift+F9
Sort... Alt+F9
Outline
Hypertext
List
Index
Cross-Reference
Table of Contents
Table of Authorities
Generate... Ctrl+F9

Graphics menu

g.

Graphics
Figure
Text
Equation
Custom Box...
Edit Box Shift+F11
Draw...
Chart...
TextArt...
Horizontal Line Ctrl+F11
Vertical Line Ctrl+Shift+F11
Custom Line...
Edit Line...
Graphics Styles...

Table menu

h.

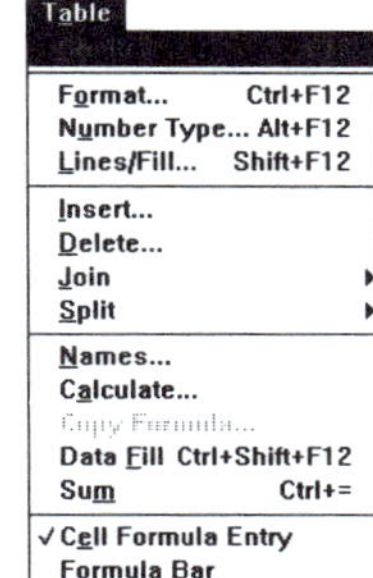

Windows menu

i.

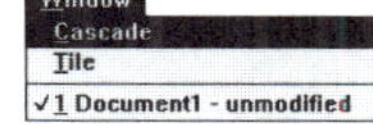

Help menu

j.

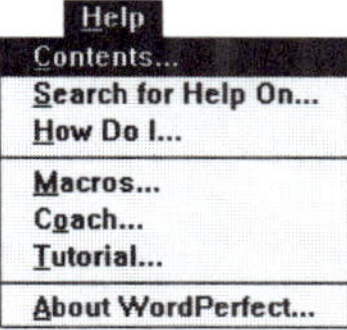

Figure 1 WordPerfect for Windows menu structure (*cont.*)

Cascading Menus

Cascading or additional menus are displayed when you choose an option that is followed by the triangle pointer (▶). You can make choices in these menus the same way you make choices in other menus. The options in these menus also have ellipses (...) or triangle pointers, following those that have additional menus or dialog boxes attached.

Choosing Options

Menus and dialog boxes both contain options that are selected, turned on, or checked to use the various WordPerfect features. You can use either the mouse or the keyboard to choose options in menus and dialog boxes.

Using the Mouse

Follow these steps to use the mouse for choosing options:

1. Click with the left mouse button on the menu item that you want. A cascading menu is displayed.
2. Click on the item in the cascading menu that you want.
3. Respond to the screen, depending on whether another menu or a dialog box is displayed.
4. When finished, you can either click on OK to complete the function or click on Cancel. In cascading menus, just click anywhere outside the menu to return to the document window without performing the function.

Using the Keyboard

Follow these steps to use the keyboard for choosing options:

1. Press ALT to make the menu bar active—the Control-menu box will become shaded. Then press the underlined character in the option you want. For example, to choose Layout, press ALT+L.

2. Press the underlined character shown in the menu item that you want, or press UP ARROW or DOWN ARROW to select it, and press ENTER. Either a dialog box or a cascading menu will be displayed, or a function or command will be executed.
3. Respond to the prompts. To move around in a dialog box, press the TAB key to move from one item to another, or press ALT and the underlined character to go directly to the item you want. Then, if necessary, press any appropriate arrow key to move from one selection to another in a list box. In some menus or dialog boxes, merely selecting the item will turn it on, and it can be turned off by selecting it again. An item is turned on when a *check mark* is shown in front of it, when an X is displayed in a check box, or when a *dot* is shown in a radio button.
4. When finished, press ENTER to complete the function, or press ESC to cancel and return to the document window without completing the function.

Using Shortcut Keys

You can use shortcut keys rather than the menu to perform some frequently used functions. For example, press F5 to print a document rather than choosing File, Print. In the menus the shortcut keys are named following the options to which they have been assigned; for example, the shortcut keys for File, Exit are Alt+F4. See the "Appendix" for the list of shortcut keys.

Creating a Document

Creating a document includes entering and editing text, tables, and graphics. It also can include formatting with appropriate margins and line spacing; adding character attributes such as bold, underlining, and italic; running spell checks; using the thesaurus; and searching and replacing text and formatting.

Entering Text

Let wordwrap work for you when you enter text in the document window. *Wordwrap* allows you to type text without pressing ENTER at the ends of lines in paragraphs. As you type, when the right margin is reached, lines are ended automatically, and text is moved to the beginning of the next line. You do, however, need to press ENTER to end paragraphs or to end short lines (such as addresses, salutations, and so on). Also press ENTER to insert blank lines in the text.

Moving Around in the Document

The term *insertion point* is used in most Windows applications in place of the term *cursor*. The insertion point is identified by a blinking vertical line. The exact page, line, and horizontal position of the insertion point is displayed at the right end of the status bar. The "Ln" (Line) number is the distance from the top of the paper. The "Pos" (Position) number is the distance from the left side of the paper.

You can use either the mouse or the keyboard to move the insertion point to any position within the text area.

Using the Mouse

In the typing area of the document window, the mouse pointer is a vertical bar that looks like a large I bar. In other areas, the pointer becomes an arrow. When working with the mouse, be careful to hold the mouse still when you click the button. You won't get the results you want if the mouse is moved when you click. The following lists the mouse actions for moving around in a document.

Type of Movement	Mouse Action
Insertion point	Point to the position you want and click the left mouse button.
Viewing window up or down one line	Click on the up or down arrows in the vertical scroll bar at the right side of the window.

Type of Movement	Mouse Action
Viewing window from one page to another	Click on the up or down page buttons at the bottom of the vertical scroll bar.
Scrolling the viewing window up or down	Point to the shaded box in the vertical scroll bar, hold down the left mouse button, and drag the block to a different position.
Scrolling the viewing window from left to right	Click on the left or right arrows in the horizontal scroll bar, or drag the shaded box to the left or right.

Using the Keyboard

The following table lists the key or combination of keys that can be used to move the insertion point in the current document.

Type of Movement	Key
Left one character	LEFT ARROW
Right one character	RIGHT ARROW
Up one line	UP ARROW
Down one line	DOWN ARROW
One word to the left	CTRL+LEFT ARROW
One word to the right	CTRL+RIGHT ARROW
Beginning of the line	HOME
Far left end of the line (before codes)	HOME, HOME
Right end of the line	END
Beginning of document (after codes)	CTRL+HOME
Beginning of document (before codes)	CTRL+HOME, CTRL+HOME
End of document	CTRL+END
Top of screen (then up one screen at a time)	PGUP
Bottom of screen (then down one screen at a time)	PGDN

Type of Movement	Key
Up one paragraph	CTRL+UP ARROW
Down one paragraph	CTRL+DOWN ARROW
First line on previous page	ALT+PGUP
First line on following page	ALT+PGDN

Using Go To

You can either choose Edit, Go To or press CTRL+G to display the Go To dialog box. From this dialog box you can enter the page number, bookmark, or cell that you want, or choose a new position from a list. Refer to GO TO in "Features and Commands" for complete instructions.

Selecting Text

Selecting text highlights a block of text, tables, or graphics. Then various WordPerfect features can be applied to the selection. For example, you can format it with a different font or with different paragraph indents; delete, copy, or move it to a new position; print it; save it as a separate file; or run a spell check on it.

Using the Mouse

To use the mouse for selecting text, just point to the beginning of the text to be selected, hold down the left mouse button, drag to the end of the text, and release the button. The selected text will be highlighted. Refer to SELECT TEXT in "Features and Commands" for more information.

Using the Keyboard

To select text using the keyboard, move the insertion point to the beginning of the text to be selected, hold down the SHIFT key, and press the arrow keys to move to the end of the text to highlight it. The word "Select" in the status bar becomes bold when you are in Select mode. Refer to SELECT TEXT in "Features and Commands" for a list of keystroke combinations that can be used to quickly select blocks of text.

Editing Text

Editing text includes deleting existing text, inserting new text, typing over old text, or moving or copying text to a different position in the document.

Inserting New Text

New text can be typed at any position in the document by moving the insertion point to the place where you want to enter it, and typing. Any existing text to the right of the insertion point will move automatically to the right and down the page to make room for the inserted text.

Deleting Text

You can either delete text one character at a time using the DEL or BACKSPACE keys, or you can select (highlight) a block of text and then delete it by pressing the DEL key. If you press a key other than DEL when working with selected text, that character will replace the selection.

Any one of your *last three deletions* can be restored at any position in the text by choosing Edit, Undelete. You can also choose Edit, Undo to reverse your *last edit,* including both deletions and new text; however, it must be used immediately after your edit.

Refer to DELETE in "Features and Commands" for a complete list of keystrokes that can be used to delete text. Also see UNDELETE and UNDO for further information.

Using Typeover Mode

Press the INS key to toggle Typeover mode on and off. In Typeover mode, move the insertion point to the position where you want to enter text and begin typing. Existing text will be deleted and replaced with the new text that you type. You can choose Edit, Undo or Edit, Undelete to restore text that is deleted in Typeover mode.

The typing mode that is currently in effect is indicated in the status bar. *Insert* is the default and is displayed when you open a new document window. When you press the INS key, the word "Typeover" replaces "Insert" in the status bar until you press the INS key again to return to Insert mode.

Formatting Text

Formatting text refers to changing the appearance of the text or changing the way it is displayed or positioned on the page. Formatting can include setting margins; changing line spacing and alignment (center, right flush, justified, and so on); applying character attributes to text, such as bold, underlining, and italic; changing font types and sizes; using multiple columns; and creating tables. Formatting characteristics are located in the Layout menu, or they can be applied from buttons in the Power bar, Button bar, or Ruler bar. Refer to the specific types of formatting in "Features and Commands."

Formatting can be applied to a document either by entering the formatting characteristics as you go, or by adding them later. If you add formatting after text has been entered, you must *select* the portion of the document that you want to change and then apply the formatting. Or if a code for the formatting is placed automatically, you move the insertion point to an appropriate position and apply formatting without selecting text. For example, when you change line spacing, move the insertion point to any position in the line and change the formatting. When done, a line spacing code will be placed automatically at the beginning of that line. In the "Features and Commands" section, when instructions are given for moving the insertion point to any position in a line, paragraph, or page, this indicates that the formatting code will be placed automatically.

Note *Codes are placed automatically when formatting for lines, paragraphs, pages, or documents is applied. Depending upon the formatting, the code for the formatting will be automatically placed at the beginning of the line, paragraph, page, or document.*

Naming and Saving a Document

Saving a document writes the text to disk, and requires that the document be given a name consisting of one to eight characters. You cannot use a space in the name, but you can use letters, numbers, or any of the following symbols:

^ ' { } - ( ) & % $ # @ !

An optional extension can be added to the filename by typing a period (.) and one to three characters. This can be used to further identify the file. WordPerfect adds the extension *.wpd* automatically if an extension is not typed with the filename.

After a document has been named and saved, additional text and edits should be saved about every 15 or 20 minutes to protect against losing your work due to a power outage or some other problem. You can also save automatically by setting a timed backup. Refer to BACKUP in "Features and Commands."

To name a document follow these steps:

1. Choose File, Save As, or click on the Save button, or press F3.
2. Type the filename that you want to use.
3. Choose OK or press ENTER.

To save a document that has already been named:

1. Choose File, Save, or click on the Save button, or press CTRL+S.

Printing a Document

You can either print a document that is in the active window, or you can print a document that is stored on the disk and not opened. See PRINT in "Features and

Commands" for details on printing a document from disk as well as other print choices.

1. Open the document to be printed.
2. Choose File, Print, or click on the Print button, or press F5.
3. Choose any of the print options that you want.
4. Choose Print.

Closing a Document

Closing a document removes it from the WordPerfect window. To do this:

1. Choose File, Close, or double-click on the Control-menu box at the left end of the title bar, or press CTRL+F4. If the document has been named and the last edits saved, the document will be cleared from the WordPerfect window.
2. If the document has not been saved previously, respond to the screen prompts to either save or not. If you choose to save, appropriate dialog boxes will be displayed depending on whether or not the document has already been named.

Refer to CLOSING A DOCUMENT WINDOW in "Features and Commands."

Opening a Document

You can open an existing document or open a new blank document window. Up to nine different document windows can be opened at the same time.

Opening an Existing Document

Opening a document is the process of displaying in a WordPerfect window a document that has previously been saved to disk.

1. Choose File, Open, or click on the Open button, or press CTRL+O. A dialog box showing the list of files is displayed.
2. Select the file to be opened from the list, or type the filename in the text box.
3. Choose OK or press ENTER.

Opening a New Document

Opening a new document displays a blank document window where you can enter and edit text.

1. Choose File, New, or click on the New Document button, or press CTRL+N. The title bar now shows [Document #]. When you save the document, the document number will be replaced with the new filename.

Working with Multiple WordPerfect Documents

Each open document is in a *document window*, and all document windows are placed in the *WordPerfect window*. You can use either the mouse or the keyboard to arrange and size document windows. The Window menu and the Control menu also contain the options that control arranging and sizing windows.

Using the Mouse

When a document is first opened, it is the full window size. Use any of the following to make changes to the windows:

Window Change	Mouse Action
Make the document window medium size	Click on the document restore button (the double-headed arrow) at the right end of the menu bar.

Window Change	Mouse Action
Size the document window	Point to any side or corner of the active window (the pointer becomes a double-headed arrow), hold down the left mouse button, and drag to a different size.
Make the document window full size	Click on the document maximize button (the up arrow) at the right end of the title bar.
Make the document window or the WordPerfect window an icon	Click on the document minimize button (the down arrow) at the right end of the title bar.
Open the icon	Double-click on the icon.
Make a window active	Click on the window.
Close a document window or the WordPerfect window	Double-click on the Control-menu box at the left end of the title bar.

Using the Keyboard

If you prefer to use the keyboard rather than the mouse, the Window menu and the Control menu can be used to move, size, and make a window active.

Using the Window Menu

You can use this menu to select the document that you want to be active or to rearrange the open windows in either a tile or cascade arrangement. The options are as follows:

Option	Result or Action
Cascade	Stacks windows so they are overlapping. Only the title bar of each is displayed.
Tile	Arranges the windows so they are not overlapping. The arrangement depends upon the number of windows that are opened.

Option	Result or Action
List of opened files	Press the number in front of the filename to select it and make it active.

Note *You can also make a document window active by pressing* CTRL+F6 *to move from one document window to another.*

Using the Control Menu
Every document window, as well as the WordPerfect window, has a Control-menu box at the left end of the menu bar. Press ALT+- (hyphen) to go to the Control menu in the active document window. Press ALT+SPACEBAR to go to the Control menu in the WordPerfect window. The options are as follows:

Option	Result
Restore	Makes the window medium size.
Move	Moves the window to a different position. A four-sided arrow will be displayed. Press the arrow keys to move the window, and when the window is placed where you want it, press ENTER.
Size	Changes the size of the window. A four-sided arrow will be displayed. Press the arrow keys to make the window a different size, and when the window is the size you want it, press ENTER.
Minimize	Makes the window an icon. You can then choose either Restore or Maximize to change the icon to a document window.
Maximize	Makes the window full size.
Close	Clears the active window from the WordPerfect window.
Next	Makes the next window active. This is not available in the WordPerfect Control menu.

Note *The Switch To option in the WordPerfect Control menu is discussed in the next section.*

Moving Between WordPerfect and Other Windows Applications

One of the advantages of using WordPerfect for Windows, is that other Windows applications can be loaded, and you can easily switch from one application to another.

There are two ways to move from one application to another. Here is one way:

1. Press ALT+TAB to display a box showing the next application.
2. Continue to hold down ALT and press and release the TAB key to cycle through all the current applications that are running.
3. When you see the one you want, release the keys.

Another way to move from one application to another is

1. Press ALT+SPACEBAR to display the Control menu for the WordPerfect window.
2. Choose Switch To. The Task List dialog box shows the applications that are currently running. Select the application you want.
3. Choose Switch To.
4. Use the arrows keys to select the desired application and press ENTER.

Note *You can also press* CTRL+ESC *to go directly to the Task List dialog box.*

Using Help

WordPerfect offers on-line help that can be accessed from any window, menu, or dialog box. Press F1 to display context-sensitive help, or choose Help from the menu bar and then select options from a list of items. You can search for a topic in an index, look at information about keystrokes for various functions, find answers to commonly asked questions, and display a glossary.

Refer to HELP in "Features and Commands" for more information.

Understanding Default Settings

When you start WordPerfect, some settings are already in effect. These are called *default* settings. Some of these settings are 8 1/2 by 11 paper size; 1-inch margins on all sides; tab stops set every 1/2 inch; single spacing; left justification; and hyphenation off. Other defaults determine the way information is shown in a window; set paths where various WordPerfect files are located; set an automatic backup; control printing; determine the keyboard being used; and specify whether or not a document summary is displayed.

Some of these settings, such as paper size or line spacing, can be changed for the current document and will be reset to the original settings in the next document; or you can make these document formatting changes permanent in the Standard template. Other defaults can be changed permanently by choosing File, Preferences.

Refer to PREFERENCES and TEMPLATE in "Features and Commands" for further information.

Exiting WordPerfect for Windows

When you are ready to leave WordPerfect, use the Exit option in the File menu. In addition to ending a word processing session, this option also allows you to save any documents that have not already been saved. This includes documents that have not been named, as well as those that have been saved previously but have not had the last edits saved.

1. Choose File, Exit, or double-click on the WordPerfect window Control-menu box, or press ALT+F4. If any open documents have been modified and the changes have not been saved, or if any open documents have not been named, you will be prompted for each to save or not.
2. Respond to the prompts for each document.
3. When all documents have been saved (or not saved), the system returns to Windows.

Features and Commands

This section presents the WordPerfect for Windows features and functions in alphabetical order for quick reference. The procedure for using the feature or function is given, followed by a brief description and explanation of its use or purpose.

ABBREVIATIONS

Abbreviations are used to save text that you type frequently, such as a return address, logo, complimentary close, and technical or foreign phrases. After creating the abbreviation, you then can *expand* it, which inserts the saved text at the insertion point.

Creating an Abbreviation

1. Type the text to be saved and select it.
2. Choose Insert, Abbreviations, Create.
3. Type a name for the abbreviation in the text box.
4. Choose OK or press ENTER.
5. Choose Close to return to the document.

Stores the saved abbreviation in the template that is currently being used.

Expanding an Abbreviation

1. Move the insertion point to the place where you want to insert the abbreviation.
2. Choose Insert, Abbreviations.
3. Select the abbreviation to be expanded from the list.
4. Choose Expand.

Shortcut Keys

1. Type a name for the abbreviation at the insertion point.
2. Press CTRL+A to expand.

Inserts the full text of the abbreviation at the insertion point in the document.

Copying an Abbreviation

1. Choose Insert, Abbreviations, Copy.
2. Select the template to copy from.
3. Select the abbreviation to be copied.
4. Select the template to copy to.
5. Choose Copy.
6. Choose Close.

Copies an abbreviation from one template to another. You do not necessarily have to be using the template in which the abbreviation is stored in order to copy it. The templates are selected in the Copy Abbreviation dialog box.

Deleting an Abbreviation

1. Choose Insert, Abbreviations.
2. Select the abbreviation.
3. Choose Delete.
4. Choose Yes.
5. Choose Close.

Removes abbreviations from the current template.

ADVANCE

1. Move the insertion point to the position where you want to enter an advance code.
2. Choose Layout, Typesetting, Advance.
3. If you want to move the text following the insertion point horizontally, choose one of the horizontal positions.
4. Enter a measurement in the Horizontal Distance text box or choose the measurement from the list. Leave

None turned on if you do not want to change the horizontal position.

5. If you want to move the text following the insertion point vertically, choose one of the vertical positions.
6. Enter a measurement in the Vertical Distance text box or choose the measurement from the list. Leave None turned on if you do not want to change the vertical position.
7. Choose OK or press ENTER.

Note *If you choose From Top of Page as the vertical position, you can then turn on Text Above Position, which positions text above the measurement. If it is turned off, the text is positioned below the measurement.*

Positions text at a specific location in relation to the insertion point or in relation to the top or left edge of the paper. This feature is frequently used to place graphics on a page or to place text when filling in a form.

APPEND

1. Select the text or graphic to be appended.
2. Choose Edit, Append.

Inserts a copy of the selected text at the end of the existing Clipboard contents, which have been placed there when you use Cut or Copy. If there are no previous Clipboard contents, or if the Clipboard contains graphics, you will not be able to choose Append.

The appended text remains in the Clipboard until you exit from Windows or choose a different item to cut or copy. If you exit from WordPerfect, the contents remain and can be used in other applications.(*See also* INSERT FILE for information about adding, appending, a file to another file.)

BACKUP

Setting a Timed Backup

1. Choose File, Preferences, File.
2. Be sure Documents/Backup is selected.
3. Change Default Directory if necessary.
4. Enter a name for a different directory to store the backup files, if you like.
5. Choose Timed Document Backup every.
6. Enter number of minutes or choose from the list.
7. Choose OK or press ENTER.
8. Choose Close to return to the document window.

Saves text automatically at the intervals specified in the dialog box. The saved backup files are named WP{WP}.BK*n* (where *n* is the number of the document window). When you exit from WordPerfect for Windows, these files are deleted; however, if you have a power outage or a system failure, they are saved. Then when you start up again, a message will be displayed telling you that backup files exist, and you can choose either Rename, and give the backup file a new name; Open, to display the file in the document window; or Delete, which will delete the file permanently.

Turning on an Original Backup

1. Choose File, Preferences, File.
2. Choose Original Document Backup to turn it on.
3. Choose OK or press ENTER.
4. Choose Close to return to the document window.

Saves the original version of the document that is open. For example, if you have made edits to the document and saved the new version, you can still get your original document back. With Original Document Backup turned on, the original document is saved using the same filename, with the extension .BK!. To retrieve your original document, open the file with the .BK! extension and rename it. Choose Backup Directory and enter a directory name if you want to save the backup files in a different directory.

BAR CODES

Placing a Bar Code on an Envelope

Keyboard

1. Choose Layout, Envelope to place a bar code on an envelope.
2. Select an envelope size.

   Note *If a paper definition for an envelope has not been created previously, you will be prompted to do that. Respond to the dialog boxes that are displayed. When you are done the Envelope dialog box will be displayed and you can proceed with the following steps.*
3. Type a return address and a mailing address, including ZIP codes, in the appropriate text boxes.
4. Choose Options and select Include USPS POSTNET Bar Code to turn it on. An X should be in the box.
5. Choose OK or press ENTER to return to the Envelope dialog box.
6. Choose POSTNET Bar Code. The mailing address ZIP code is then displayed in the POSTNET Bar Code text box.
7. You can then choose Print Envelope to print and to return to the document.

Note *Once the Include USPS POSTNET Bar Code is turned on, it remains on until you turn it off. If it is turned on, you can skip steps 4 and 5 above, and just click in the POSTNET Bar Code text box to display the ZIP code number.*

Mouse

1. Click the Envelope button in the Button Bar. Then follow the preceding steps 2 through 7 for placing a bar code on an envelope.

Places a POSTNET bar code on an envelope, which helps speed up mail sorting. You can insert the bar code for either a 5-digit ZIP code, a ZIP code plus the 4-digit codes, or an 11-digit code.

Placing a Bar Code in a Document or in Labels

1. Move the insertion point to the place in the document where the bar code is to be inserted; or choose Layout, Labels, choose the label type, choose Select, and move the insertion point to the place where the bar code is to be inserted.
2. Choose Insert, Other, Bar Code.
3. Type the ZIP code number in the Bar Code Digits text box.
4. Choose OK or press ENTER.

Inserts a bar code at any position in a document or labels (*see also* ENVELOPES).

Note *Bar codes can be deleted by moving the insertion point to the end of the code and pressing BACKSPACE.*

BASELINE PLACEMENT

1. Choose Layout, Typesetting, Word/Letterspacing.
2. Choose Baseline Placement for Typesetting.
3. Choose OK or press ENTER.

Sets the first baseline on the page *even* with the top margin. The baseline is the line upon which the bottom of the characters is placed. The default is for the top margin to be even with the top of the characters, which means the baseline will vary depending upon the font size. When Baseline Placement is turned on, the baseline, which is now even with the top margin, is always the same regardless of the font size, and allows precise placement of text in the document.

BINDING

Formatting a Document with Page Binding

1. Choose Layout, Page, Binding.
2. Choose the side of the page where the margin is to be increased to allow for binding.
3. Specify the amount of increase in width in the Amount text box, or click on the arrows to select a measurement.
4. Choose the Duplexing option if your printer prints double-sided, or if you want to print pages that can be copied double-sided.
5. If the duplexing is turned on, choose From Long Edge if you are going to bind the pages at the 11-inch side or From Short Edge if you are going to bind the pages at the 8 1/2-inch side.
6. Choose OK or press ENTER.

Prints pages with one margin wider than the opposite margin to accommodate binding. If you choose duplexing, the wider margin for the binding is placed on alternating pages in the document. The binding width will be shown in the document window as a shaded band. Choose View, Two Page to see duplexing.

Printing Pages To Be Bound

1. Choose File, Print. (Or press F5.)
2. Choose Options.
3. Choose Booklet Printing.
4. Choose OK.
5. Choose Print.

Prints documents that are formatted with extra width for bindings. Use this only if your printer is capable of printing on both sides of the paper.

BLOCK PROTECT

1. Select the text.
2. Choose Layout, Page, Keep Text Together.
3. Choose Keep selected text together on same page.
4. Choose OK or press ENTER.

Keeps a block of text on one page as long as the block is not more than one page in length. This can be used to prevent a page break within a table, for example. The text that is block protected can be bumped to the next page if there is not enough room for it on the current page (*see also* CONDITIONAL END OF PAGE).

BOLD

Keyboard

1. Choose Layout, Font, Bold and press ENTER. (Or press CTRL+B.)
2. Type the text.
3. Choose Layout, Font, Bold and press ENTER to end the formatting. (Or press CTRL+B again.)

Mouse

1. Click the Bold Font button in the Power Bar. It is depressed when selected.
2. Type the text.
3. Click the Bold Font button to end formatting.

Makes text darker than normal. Boldface is generally used to call attention to or add emphasis to specific text.

Note *You can apply bold to text after it has been typed by selecting the text and then clicking on the Bold Font button in the Power Bar, by pressing CTRL+B, or by choosing Layout, Font, Bold.*

BOOKMARK

A bookmark is used to mark a position in the document that you may want to locate later. It can be at a specific place, or it can be a block of text. You can have as many bookmarks as you need in a document. This is different from a Quickmark in that a Quickmark is limited to only one per document (*see also* QUICKMARK).

Creating a Bookmark

1. Move the insertion point to the position where you want to place the bookmark, or select a block of text that is to be the bookmark.
2. Choose Insert, Bookmark, Create.
3. Type a name and choose OK or press ENTER.

Places a bookmark in the document that can be used to move quickly to that position. If you add a bookmark name to a block of text, this text can be located quickly and moved, copied, or deleted.

Finding a Bookmark

1. Choose Insert, Bookmark.
2. Select the bookmark name that you want to locate and choose Go To.

Moves the insertion point quickly to the text that was designated as a bookmark.

Note *Other options in the Bookmark dialog box can be used to* move, rename, *and* delete *a bookmark name. The Go To & Select option goes to the bookmark text and highlights it. Choose Insert, Bookmark, select the bookmark* *name, and then choose the option you want. Respond to the prompts, depending upon the option you choose.*

BORDERS

Adding Paragraph Borders

1. Place the insertion point at any position in the paragraph.
2. Choose Layout, Paragraph, Border/Fill.
3. Choose Border Style. Press the spacebar or click the Border Style button to display examples.
4. Choose the style you want. Either press the arrow keys to go to the style in the example box and press ENTER, or click on the example of the style you want.

Note *You can also choose Border Style, and press the up or down arrow to select a style; or click on the arrows at the end of the text box, and select a style from the list.*

5. Choose Fill Style if you want to select a foreground or background color. Press the spacebar or click the Fill Style button to display examples.
6. Choose the shade and pattern. Either press the arrow keys to go to the example in the example box and press ENTER, or click on the example of the shade and pattern that you want.
7. If you selected a Fill style, choose Foreground and a different color if you like.
8. If you selected a Fill style, choose Background and a different color if you like.
9. Choose OK or press ENTER.

Adds a border around the paragraph in which the insertion point is located. When ENTER is pressed at the end of the paragraph, the border increases in size to include additional paragraphs.

Note *A separator line can be inserted between paragraphs. Place the insertion point in the first paragraph, choose Layout, Paragraph, Border/Fill, Border Style and choose Column Between from the drop-down list. A separator line will be added below the paragraph. When you press ENTER at the end of the first paragraph, additional separator lines are inserted below it. Horizontal lines appear after pressing ENTER for all subsequent paragraphs.*

Adding Page Borders

1. Place the insertion point at any position on the page.
2. Choose Layout, Page, Border/Fill.
3. Choose Border Style. Click the button to display examples or select from the list. *See* step 3 in "Adding Paragraph Borders."
4. Select the style from the list. *See* step 4 in "Adding Paragraph Borders."
5. Choose Fill Style if you want to add a fill to either the foreground or background. Click the button to display examples. *See* step 5 and 6 in "Adding Paragraph Borders."
6. Choose Foreground or Background—either one or both—and select a pattern or color.
7. Choose OK or press ENTER.

Adds a border around the entire page. All following pages will have a border until you turn the Border feature off.

Adding Column Borders

1. Place the insertion point at any position in the column.
2. Choose Layout, Columns, Border/Fill.
3. Choose Border Style and press the DOWN ARROW or click on the arrow button to display the drop-down list.
4. Select Column Between to place a border between columns only; or select Column All to place a border around the outside edge as well as between columns.
5. Choose Fill Style and select a style you want.
6. Choose Foreground or Background, if you like, and select a color or pattern.

7. Choose OK or press ENTER.

Inserts a border either between columns or between columns and also around the outside edges.

Turning Off Borders

1. Place the insertion point in the paragraph, page, or column.
2. Choose Layout and Paragraph, Page, or Columns.
3. Choose Border/Fill.
4. Choose Off.

Discontinues formatting the text with borders.

Customizing Borders

1. Place the insertion point in the paragraph, page, or column that contains the border to be customized.
2. Choose Layout, then Paragraph, Page, or Columns.
3. Choose Border/Fill.
4. Choose a border style.
5. Choose Customize Style.
6. Make the changes you want in the Customize Border dialog box.
7. Choose OK, then choose OK again to return to the document window.

Changes the border style in effect at the insertion point. Changes can include selecting a different style, changing the line style, adjusting spacing inside and outside the border, changing colors, adding shadows, changing corner style (only for page borders), changing the thickness of lines, and setting a fill style for inside the border (*see also* GRAPHICS).

BOXES

See GRAPHICS

BULLETED AND NUMBERED LISTS

Keyboard

1. Move the insertion point to the place where you want to begin entering bullets.
2. Choose Insert, Bullets & Numbers.
3. Select the bullet or number style from the Styles list box.
4. Choose New Bullet or Number on ENTER.
5. Press ENTER.

Mouse

1. Move the insertion point to the place where you want to begin entering bullets.
2. Click the Bullets & Numbers button in the Button Bar. Then follow the preceding steps 3 through 5.

Shortcut Keys

1. If you did not turn on New Bullet or Number on ENTER, you can press CTRL+SHIFT+B to insert a bullet, which is the default, or if you selected numbered list, then press CTRL+SHIFT+B to insert the next number.

Adds bullets or numbers at the beginning of each paragraph. If you choose a number style in the Style list box, you can also select and change the starting value for numbering. The default is "1"; however, you can change this to any value you want. Just press the UP ARROW or click on the up arrow button and select the number you want.

Note *You can also add bullets to paragraphs after text has been typed. Select the paragraphs and click the Bullet button, or choose Insert, Bullets & Numbers, then select the bullets or numbers style you want to apply and choose OK. If you press CTRL+SHIFT+B, the style that is selected in the Bullets & Numbers dialog box will be applied* (see also *OUTLINING*).

BUTTON BAR

Moving the Button Bar

Mouse

1. Point to any border or shaded area. The pointer becomes a hand.
2. Hold down the left mouse button and drag the outline to a different location. The hand becomes an outline when you start dragging.
3. Release the mouse button.

Moves the Button Bar to a different location and also changes its shape. You can size the Button Bar window the same way you size other windows: Point to any side or corner (the pointer becomes a double-sided arrow), and drag to a different size.

To return the Button Bar to its original size and position in the window, point to any shaded area to show the hand. Then hold down the left mouse button, drag the window up until the outline becomes the original size of the Button Bar, and release the mouse button.

Removing the Button Bar

Keyboard

1. Choose View, Button Bar. (The check mark is removed from in front of Button Bar.)

Mouse

1. Click the View Button Bar button in the Power Bar.

Increases the size of the viewing window by removing the button bar.

If you repositioned the Button Bar, you can click the Close button at the left end of the title bar to remove it from the window. (*See also* HIDE BARS.)

CASE

Using Caps Lock

1. Press CAPS LOCK to turn on uppercase.
2. Type text.
3. Press CAPS LOCK to turn off uppercase.

Enters all alphabet characters in uppercase. If you press the SHIFT key when you type a letter, it will be in lowercase. Numbers and symbols are not affected by CAPS LOCK. To type the symbols that are on the number keys, press the SHIFT key and the number, as you normally do.

Formatting Text as Small Caps

Keyboard

1. Move the insertion point to the position where you want to begin formatting characters as small capital letters.
2. Choose Layout, Font. (Or press F9 to open the Font dialog box.)
3. Select Small Cap.
4. Press ENTER.
5. Type the text.
6. Choose Layout, Font, Small Cap to end the formatting.

Mouse

1. Move the insertion point to the position where you want to begin formatting characters as small capital letters.
2. Click the right mouse button to display the QuickMenu and choose Font. Then follow the preceding steps 3 through 6.

Formats characters as uppercase letters but the same size as lowercase letters.

Note *You can also format text as small caps after it has been typed by selecting the text and choosing Layout, Font, Small Cap.*

Converting Case

1. Select the text.
2. Choose Edit, Convert Case.
3. Choose either Lowercase, Uppercase, or Initial Capitals.

Changes the selected text quickly to upper- or lowercase, or formats the text with only the first character of each word in uppercase. This is a very quick way of formatting a large block of text. For example, if a table of contents has been generated from headings in text, and all of the headings are in uppercase, you may want to change them to initial capitals or to lowercase for the table of contents.

Note *You can also select a block of text and press CTRL+K to change text to uppercase or to lowercase. The initial capitals option is not available when you do this.*

CENTERING

Centering a Page

1. Place the insertion point at any position on the page.
2. Choose Layout, Page, Center.
3. Choose Current Page, or Current & Subsequent Pages.
4. Choose OK or press ENTER.

Automatically centers all text on the page between the top and bottom margins. This is especially useful for announcements, ads, or other documents where the text appearance would be enhanced by centering. The code for page centering is automatically inserted at the top of the page.

If you choose Current & Subsequent Pages and want to end the formatting before you get to the end of the document, choose No Centering on the page following the last centered page.

Centering a Line of Text Between Left and Right Margins

Keyboard

1. Place the insertion point at the beginning of the line of text to be centered.
2. Choose Layout, Line, Center. (Or press SHIFT+F7.)
3. Type the text.
4. Press ENTER to end centering and go to the next line.

Mouse

1. Place the insertion point at the beginning of the line of text to be centered.
2. Click with the right mouse button at any position, to display the QuickMenu.
3. Choose Center.
4. Type the text.
5. Press ENTER to end centering and go to the next line.

Centers each line of text horizontally. The command can be entered for each line as it is typed, following the steps above; or you can type a line, move the insertion point to the beginning of the line, and apply the center command; or you can type several lines, select them, and then apply the center command.

Note *To add dot leaders in front of text that is centered, repeat keyboard or mouse steps 1 and 2 above.*

Centering Text at a Specific Position

1. Press TAB to position the cursor at a tab stop on the line.
2. Choose Layout, Line, Center. (Press SHIFT+F7 or click the right mouse button and choose Center.)
3. Type the text and press ENTER to end the centering and go to the next line.

Centers text at any tab position on the line.

Using Center Justification

Keyboard

1. Move the insertion point to the place where you want to begin centering lines.
2. Choose Layout, Justification, Center. (Or press CTRL+E.)

Mouse

1. Move the insertion point to the place where you want to begin centering lines.
2. Hold down the Justification button in the Power Bar and drag to select Center.

Centers all lines of text, including those ending with a hard return. To end center justification, press CTRL+L; or hold down the Justification button and select Left; or choose Layout, Justification, Left (or any other type of line alignment that you want).

CHARACTERS

Using Character Set

1. Move the insertion point to the place where you want to insert a WordPerfect character or symbol.
2. Choose Insert, Character. (Or press CTRL+W.)
3. Choose Character Set and display the list of sets.
4. Select the set that contains the character you want.
5. Choose Characters and select the character you want; or if you know the character's number, enter it in the Number text box.
6. Choose Insert if you want to insert additional characters; choose Insert and Close if you are selecting only one character or if you are inserting the last character; choose Close to leave the dialog box.

Inserts special characters in the document. Some characters may not be displayed in the window—a box will show in place of the character. In Reveal Codes, a code will show the number of the character that has been inserted.

Note *WordPerfect provides 15 sets, totaling 1500 characters that can be inserted.*

Using Character Mapping

See KEYBOARD LAYOUT

CHART

Inserting a Chart

Keyboard

1. Move the insertion point to the place where you want to insert a WordPerfect chart.
2. Choose Insert, Object.
3. Select WP Chart 2.1 as the Object Type.
4. Press ENTER.

Mouse

1. Move the insertion point to the place where you want to insert a WordPerfect chart.
2. Click the Chart button in the Button Bar.

Goes to the WP Draw window. The sample table in the Draw window shows data and the corresponding chart that is created on the basis of that data. You can delete the items in the table and enter your own information. The chart will be created automatically based on that new information. Use the options in the menu bar to edit the chart. (The title bar explains or provides a description of each item as you point to it.) You can also click the buttons in the palette at the left to make changes. In addition, the bar at the bottom of the Draw window contains buttons that are used to return to the document, update the chart, or redraw the chart.

Returning to WordPerfect

Keyboard

1. Choose File, Exit & Return to Document.
2. Choose Yes to save changes to the document in WordPerfect.

Mouse

1. Click the Return button at the bottom of the Draw window; or double-click on the Control-menu box at the left end of the menu bar. Then follow the preceding step 2.

Saves the chart edits and returns to the WordPerfect document window. The chart is entered at the insertion point.

Editing a Chart

Keyboard

1. Choose Graphics, Edit Box. (Or press SHIFT+F11.) If more than one graphic exists, choose the box number for the chart and press ENTER.
2. Choose Edit, WP Chart 2.1 Object, Edit.
3. Make any changes.
4. Choose File, Exit & Return to Document.
5. Choose Yes to save changes to the document in WordPerfect.

Mouse

1. Double-click the chart in the document window.
2. Make any changes.
3. Click the Return button at the bottom of the Draw window, or double-click on the Control-menu box at the left end of the menu bar. Choose Yes to save changes and return to the WordPerfect document window.

Edits the chart using the same general procedures used for creating the chart. The menu is the same, and the features can be added and changed in the same way they were entered or changed originally.

CLIPBOARD CONTENTS

1. Press ALT+TAB until the Program Manager box is displayed. Release the keys.
2. Double-click the Main group icon if it is not opened.
3. Double-click the Clipboard Viewer icon to open it and see the contents.

Displays the current contents of the Clipboard. They may include selections from WordPerfect or from other Windows applications that have been cut to the Clipboard. Each time you cut text, the previous contents of the Clipboard are deleted and replaced with the current selection unless you choose Append (*see* APPEND). When Append is chosen, the previous contents will remain in the Clipboard and additional text is added at the end.

Leaving the Clipboard Open and Returning to the WordPerfect Window

1. Press ALT+TAB until the box containing the WordPerfect document name is displayed. (Or click anywhere in the document window.)
2. Release the keys.

Leaves the Clipboard open and returns to the WordPerfect window. The next time you want to see the contents, press ALT+TAB until the Clipboard Viewer box is displayed and release the keys; or press CTRL+ESC, select Clipboard Viewer from the Task List, and choose Switch To.

Closing the Clipboard and Returning to the WordPerfect Window

Keyboard

1. Choose File, Exit.

Mouse

1. Double-click the Control-menu box at the left end of the title bar.

Closes the Clipboard and returns to the WordPerfect document window.

CLOSING A DOCUMENT WINDOW

Keyboard

1. Choose File, Close. (Or press CTRL+F4.)

Mouse

1. Double-click the Control-menu box at the left end of the menu bar in the document window.

Closes the active document window. If the document has not been saved previously, a dialog box will be displayed asking if you want to save. If you choose to save, a second dialog box will be displayed where you can name the document, or save edits if the document is already named.

Note *Press CTRL+SHIFT+F4 to close without saving the document.*

COACH

1. Choose Help, Coach.
2. Select the type of lesson you want.

3. Choose OK or press ENTER.

Guides you through the steps required for completing the selected task. This is an efficient way of learning the WordPerfect procedures for features such as merge, macros, and graphics, as well as all the other WordPerfect functions.

CODES

See INITIAL CODES, OTHER CODES, or REVEAL CODES

COLOR

Formatting in Color

Keyboard

1. Move the insertion point to the place where you want to change color.
2. Choose Layout, Font. (Or press F9.)
3. Choose Color and select the color you want from the palette.
4. Choose Shading and enter a percent of 100, or select from the list.
5. Choose the Palette button if you want to define colors. Enter a name and change the settings. Choose Save As to save the palette for use later, or choose OK when done.
6. Choose OK or press ENTER.

Mouse

1. Move the insertion point to the place where you want to change color.
2. Click the right mouse button and choose Font. Then follow the preceding steps 3 through 6.

Changes the color and shading for the text from the insertion point on, until you use these same steps to change it again.

Selecting a Printer for Color Printing

1. Choose File, Select Printer.
2. Choose Printers and select the color printer you want.
3. Choose Select.

Selects a color printer if one is available to you. You may not have to do this if it is already selected.

Printing in Color

Keyboard

1. Choose File, Print. (Or press F5.)
2. Select Print Color.
3. Choose Print.

Mouse

1. Click the Print button in the Power Bar. Then follow the preceding steps 2 and 3.

Prints the document in color.

Note *The Print Color option will not be available if a color printer is not selected.*

Setting a Default Palette

1. Choose File, Preferences, Print (press ENTER when the Print icon is selected, or double-click on it).
2. Choose Define Color Printing Palette.
3. Choose Open.
4. Select a palette.
5. Choose OK enough times to return to the Preferences dialog box.
6. Choose Close.

Changes the default colors that are used for a color printer. If you have defined palettes, you can select the one you want to use as a default for printing rather than selecting it each time you print. (*See* "Formatting in Color" for defining a palette.)

COLUMNS

Using Newspaper Columns

Keyboard

1. Move the insertion point to the place where you want to begin typing in columns.
2. Choose Layout, Columns, Define.
3. Enter the number of columns in the Columns text box or choose from the list.
4. Choose Newspaper if it is not already chosen. (It is the default.) The example box at the right shows the columns on the page.
5. If you like, change Spacing Between Columns and also change Column Widths for specific columns. The column numbers are the hot keys used to select specific columns.
6. Press ENTER.

Mouse

1. Move the insertion point to the place where you want to begin typing in columns.
2. Point to the Columns Define button in the Power Bar.
3. Hold down the left mouse button and drag to select the number of columns you want.
4. Release the mouse button.

Begins newspaper column formatting. As you type the text, it snakes from one column to the next. When done, point to the Columns Define button, hold down the left mouse button, and select Columns Off; or choose Layout, Columns, Off. The column number in which the insertion point is located is shown in the status bar.

Using Balanced Newspaper Columns

Keyboard

1. Move the insertion point to the place where you want to begin typing in columns.
2. Choose Layout, Columns, Define.
3. Enter the number of columns or choose from the list.
4. Choose Balanced Newspaper. The example box at the right shows how the columns will look.
5. If you like, change Spacing Between Columns and change Column Widths. The column numbers are the hot keys that can be pressed to select specific columns.
6. Choose OK or press ENTER.

Mouse

1. Move the insertion point to the place where you want to begin typing in columns.
2. Double-click the Columns Define button in the Power Bar. Then follow the preceding steps 3 through 6.

Makes all newspaper columns equal in length. As you type the text, it will be automatically divided so that all columns are equal. To end the column formatting, point to the Columns Define button, hold down the left mouse button, and select Columns Off; or choose Layout, Columns, Off.

Using Parallel Columns

Keyboard

1. Move the insertion point to the place where you want to begin typing in parallel columns.
2. Choose Layout, Columns, Define.
3. Enter the number of columns or choose from the list.
4. Select Parallel or Parallel w/Block Protect.
5. If you like, change Spacing Between Columns and change Column Widths. The column numbers

are the hot keys that can be pressed to select specific columns.

6. Choose OK or press ENTER.

Mouse

1. Move the insertion point to the place where you want to begin typing in parallel columns. Press CTRL+ENTER to move from one column to the next.
2. Double-click the Columns Define button in the Power Bar. Then follow the preceding steps 3 through 6.

Keeps corresponding text together in the same row as well as formatting text in columns. This is frequently used for conference schedules or scripts, where you want to ensure that the text in column 1 is kept in the same row as the text in column 2. You can also use the table feature for this, if you prefer. (*See also* TABLES.)

Parallel w/Block Protect keeps the entire row on one page. If any column in the row has too many lines for the current page, the entire row will be moved to the next page.

Inserting Column Breaks

Keyboard

1. Move the insertion point to the place where you want to end a column.
2. Choose Layout, Columns, Column Break. (Or press CTRL+ENTER.)

Mouse

1. Move the insertion point to the place where you want to end a column.
2. Point to the Column Define button, hold down the left mouse button, and drag to select Column Break.

Moves the text that is below the break to the next column and inserts a column break line in the document. This procedure allows you to manually control the column lengths.

The column number where your insertion point is located is displayed in the status bar in all types of columns. This is helpful, especially when editing and moving from column to column.

Note *If CTRL+ENTER is pressed in the middle of a single column, which is actually a full page, a hard page break is inserted.*

COMMENTS

1. Move the insertion point to the location where you want to enter a comment.
2. Choose Insert, Comment, Create.
3. Type the comment.
4. Choose any of the following from the Comment features bar if you want to insert them in your comment: Initials, Name, Date, or Time.
5. Choose Next or Previous to see other comments that have been entered in the document.
6. Choose Close. The comment icon is displayed in the text.

Inserts instructions, comments, or other information in the document. To see the text of the comment in the document window, click the comment icon. To remove the text from the window, click at any other place in the document or press any key. *See* "Editing a Comment" and "Converting Comments to Text" for other ways of seeing the text of the comment..

Editing a Comment

1. Move the insertion point directly following the comment. Use Reveal Codes to locate the comment code. If you have only one comment, the insertion point location can be anywhere in the document.
2. Choose Insert, Comment, Edit.
3. Make the edits and choose Close.

Displays the comment text and allows you to edit it as you would edit other text. (*See also* REVEAL CODES and PAGE VIEW.)

Note *In Page view, double-click the comment icon to go directly to the text, make edits, and choose Close.*

Converting Comments to Text

1. Move the insertion point directly following the comment. Use Reveal Codes to locate the comment code.
2. Choose Insert, Comment, Convert to Text.

Removes the comment icon and displays the text of the comment in the document.

Note *You can convert text to comments by selecting the text and choosing Insert, Comment, Create.*

Printing Comments

Comments are not printed when the document is printed. If you want to print them, convert them to text; or when you create or edit a comment, you can print it from the comment window by choosing File, Print, Print.

Removing a Comment

1. To remove a comment, select the comment code and press Delete, or drag it from the Reveal Codes window.

(*See* DELETE and REVEAL CODES for instructions on deleting codes.)

CONCORDANCE

See INDEX

CONDITIONAL END OF PAGE

1. Move the insertion point to the beginning of the text to be kept together.
2. Choose Layout, Page, Keep Text Together.
3. Choose Number of lines to keep together.
4. Enter the number of lines or choose from the list. This number should include all lines of text plus blank lines.
5. Choose OK or press ENTER.

Keeps text together on one page and is frequently used to keep headings or titles on the same page with following text (*see also* BLOCK PROTECT).

CONVERTING DOCUMENT FILES

Opening a File with a Different Format

Keyboard

1. Choose File, Open. (Or press CTRL+O.)
2. Type the filename. Or double-click the directory name that contains the file, choose List Files of Type, and select the format for the file to display all files with that format.
3. Select the file you want and choose OK. A Convert File Format box will appear.
4. Choose OK or press ENTER to convert to WPWin 6.0.

Mouse

1. Click the Open button in the Power Bar. Then follow the preceding steps 2 through 4.

Converts files that have been saved in a program other than WordPerfect.

Note *The Convert File Format dialog box will not appear if you are converting files from WordPerfect 5.1 or 5.2.*

Saving a WordPerfect File in a Different Format

Keyboard

1. Choose File, Save As. (Or press F3.)
2. Enter the filename.
3. Choose Format and display the pop-up list.
4. Choose the format type that you want.
5. Choose OK or press ENTER.

Mouse

1. Click the Save button in the Power Bar. Then follow the preceding steps 2 through 5.

Saves a WordPerfect file in a format that is compatible with other programs.

COPY

Copying Text to the Clipboard

Keyboard

1. Select the text that you want to copy.
2. Choose Edit, Copy. (Or press CTRL+C.)

Mouse

1. Select the text that you want to copy.
2. Click the Copy button in the Power Bar.

Copies text to the Clipboard. The text can then be inserted at a different position in the document using Paste, or it can be inserted in other documents. The text remains in the Clipboard until another block of text is cut or copied to the Clipboard (unless you choose Append). If you exit from WordPerfect for Windows, the contents of the Clipboard remain and can be used in other applications. (*See also* APPEND.)

Copying a Document or Figure File

1. Choose one of the following: File, Open; File, Save As; Insert, File; or Graphics, Figure.
2. Select the file to be copied—be sure it is highlighted.
3. Choose File Options.
4. Choose Copy.
5. Type the drive name, the directory name, or a different filename in the To text box.
6. Choose Copy.

Copies the file to a different drive or directory; or you can copy it to a different file by giving it a different filename (*see* SELECT TEXT for selecting several files at once).

COUNTERS

Creating a Counter

1. Move the insertion point to the place where you want to begin placing counters.
2. Choose Insert, Other, Counter.
3. Choose Create.
4. Type a name in the Counter Name text box.
5. Select the method of numbering that you want from the pop-up list.
6. Specify the number of levels you want.
7. Choose OK.
8. Choose Close.

Creates a file that stores the choices you make for the type of counter. For example, counters can be used to numbered lists, tables, headings, or titles. This file can then be selected later and used elsewhere in the document or used in other documents. You can change the amounts of increments and decrements, or change the value (the default is 1) in the Counter Numbering dialog box. You can also choose Edit and in the Edit Counter Definition dialog box, change the numbering method. Choices are letters, numbers, or Roman numerals.

Displaying a Counter

1. Move the insertion point to the place where you want to insert a counter.
2. Choose Insert, Other, Counter.
3. Select the counter you want.
4. Choose Display in Document to display the same number; choose Increase and Display to display the next larger number; or choose Decrease and Display to display the next smaller number.

Places a counter (a number) at the insertion point. The counter is not inserted automatically—use the steps just given to insert a counter at each position. The supplied counters are for graphic boxes; however, they can be used for anything that you want to count in the same way that the counter that you created is used.

For example, if you want to number tables in a document, first create the counter—name it "table"—and select the type of numbering and the levels that you want Then at each table, insert a counter and choose Increase and Display to number the tables consecutively.

CROSS-REFERENCE

1. Move the insertion point to the place where you want the cross-reference.
2. Type a reference statement—for example: Refer to the illustration on page and insert a space following the last word.
3. Choose Tools, Cross-Reference to display the Cross-Reference features bar.

4. Choose Reference and choose the type from the drop-down list. Page is the default.
5. Type a target name in the Target text box. (The target is the text, illustration, table, and so on to which you are referring.) If you have already created the target, select the name from the drop-down list.
6. Choose Mark Reference. A question mark (?) will appear in the reference statement in your document.
7. Move the insertion point directly following the text, table, or other WordPerfect feature that is to be the target to link the target to the reference. (You may want to turn on Reveal Codes to locate the end of the target.)
8. If you need to display the Cross-Reference features bar again, choose Tools, Cross-Reference.
9. Type a name in the Target text box—it must be the same as the target named in the Reference—or select the name from the list if the target is already named.
10. Choose Mark Target.
11. Choose Generate and choose OK or press ENTER.
12. Choose Close to remove the Cross-Reference features bar.

Note *If you are using the keyboard, press ALT+SHIFT and the underlined character to choose an item in the Cross-Reference feature bar.*

Marks both the reference and the target, and automatically inserts a number in the reference statement.

You can insert a reference to a page, secondary page, chapter, volume, paragraph, footnote, endnote, caption, or counter. The procedures are basically the same, just choose the appropriate type of reference in the Cross-Reference features bar.

To mark a page number for a footnote or endnote, the insertion point must be in the footnote or endnote. Endnotes must be generated first so the page numbers are current.

If editing changes the location of cross-references, generate again to update the reference. For example, if additional text moves the target to a different page number, you need to generate the reference again to change the page number in the reference statement. Also, you can create more than one cross-reference on a target.

CUT

Keyboard

1. Select the text to be cut.
2. Choose Edit, Cut. (Or press CTRL+X.)

Mouse

1. Select the text to be cut.
2. Click the Cut button in the Power Bar.

Cuts the selected text to the Clipboard. The text can then be inserted at other positions in the document or in other documents using Paste (*see also* COPY).

DATABASE

See IMPORT DATA

DATE

Inserting Date Text

Keyboard

1. Move the insertion point to the place where you want to insert the current date.
2. Choose Insert, Date, Date Text. (Or press CTRL+D.)

Mouse

1. Move the insertion point to the place where you want to insert the current date.
2. Click the Date Text button in the Button Bar.

Places the current date in the document. The default format is to print the date as "January 1, 1994"; however, the format can be changed (*see* "Changing the Date Format" in this section).

Inserting a Date Code

1. Move the insertion point to the place where you want to insert the code that will print the current date.
2. Choose Insert, Date, Date Code. (Or press CTRL+SHIFT+D.)

Inserts a code at the insertion point that will display the current date whenever the document is opened. This is useful when creating form letters that are printed on different days. The current date will be displayed automatically if a date code is inserted.

Changing the Date Format

1. Move the insertion point to the place where you want to display the date in a different format.
2. Choose Insert, Date, Date Format.
3. Choose a format from the list of Predefined Formats.
4. Choose OK or press ENTER. Or choose Custom, then Date codes and select from the list, and choose Insert. You may want to delete existing codes in the Edit Date Format text box.
5. Choose Time Codes and select from the list, and choose Insert. An example will be shown at the top of the dialog box.
6. Choose OK or press ENTER.

Changes the format for inserting a date in a document. After changing the format, use the previous steps for inserting either the date or the date code.

DELAY CODES

1. Move the insertion point to any page.
2. Choose Layout, Page.
3. Choose Delay Codes.
4. Enter the number of pages you want to delay the codes.
5. Choose OK. The features bar is displayed.
6. Enter the formatting codes that are to be delayed using the WordPerfect menu bar; or use the feature bar to change paper size, insert figures, headers, footers, or watermarks.
7. Choose Close.

Places a delay code at the beginning of the document, or at a previous hard page break. The formatting codes included in the delay code will be applied at the page specified in the delay code. Delay codes are generally used to begin formatting with a different paper size, with columns or tabs, starting page numbering, or displaying a watermark on a specific page. Using delay codes allows you to enter formatting all at one time for an entire document.

If your insertion point is on page 2, and you enter **4** for the number of pages to delay, the Delay Code will indicate 6 as the page on which the formatting changes will begin. Click on the Delay code [Delay] in Reveal Codes to see the number of pages to delay.

Note *Only open codes, those with only a beginning code, can be delayed. These are codes such as margins, paper size, justification, or tab sets. Paired codes, those with beginning and ending codes, such as bold, underline, or tables, cannot be included in a delay code.*

DELETE

Keyboard

The following table lists the methods of removing text or codes from the current window with the keyboard.

To Delete	Press
Character to left	BACKSPACE
Character at the insertion point	DEL
Selected text	DEL, BACKSPACE, or any character. If you press any character, it will replace the selection.
Word at insertion point	CTRL+BACKSPACE
From insertion point to end of line	CTRL+DEL
From insertion point to end of page	CTRL+SHIFT+DEL
Codes	In Reveal Codes, move insertion point to the left of the code and press DEL; or move to the right of the code and press BACKSPACE.

Note *To restore a deletion, choose Edit, Undo or press CTRL+Z immediately after deleting.*

Mouse

The following table lists the methods of removing selected text or codes from the Reveal Codes window with the mouse.

To Delete	Mouse Action
A code in Reveal Codes	Drag the code out of the Reveal Codes window.
Selected text	Click the right mouse button and choose Delete.

Note *Click the Undo button in the Power Bar to restore the last deletion.*

See also SELECT TEXT, UNDO, UNDELETE.

Deleting Document Files

1. Open a Directory dialog box—choose File, Open; File, Save As; or Insert, File.
2. Double-click the directory to display its files. (You may have to choose the file types you want.)
3. Select the file to be deleted. Type the first letter of the filename to locate it quickly.
4. Choose File Options, Delete, Delete.

Removes document files from the selected directory. You can also use these steps to delete other files such as templates, graphics, and charts (*see* SELECT TEXT for instructions on selecting several files).

DIRECTORIES

Creating a Directory

1. Open a Directory dialog box—choose File, Open; File, Save As; or Insert, File.
2. Choose File Options, Create Directory.
3. Type a directory name.
4. Choose Create.

Creates a new directory or subdirectory. If you are currently in the WPWin60 directory, this procedure creates a subdirectory in the WPWin60 directory unless you specify a different path when you type the directory name.

Choosing a Directory

1. Open a Directory dialog box—choose File, Open; File, Save As; or Insert, File.

2. Choose the Directories list box, press the DOWN ARROW to select the directory you want, and press ENTER; or double-click the directory name.

Displays the directory name above the Directories list box.

Making a Directory the Default Directory

1. Choose File, Preferences, File.
2. Choose Documents/Backup if it is not already turned on.
3. Type the directory name for document files in the Default Directory text box, or click on the button at the right end of the text box and select a directory name.
4. If you like, specify a default extension in the Use Default Extension on Open and Save text box. Otherwise, .wpd is the extension that is added when a document is saved.
5. Choose OK, and then choose Close to return to the document.

Designates the default directory, which means that all subsequent documents will be stored there.

Deleting a Directory

1. Open a Directory dialog box—choose File, Open; File, Save As; or Insert, File.
2. Select the directory to be deleted.
3. Choose File Options, Remove Directory.
4. Choose Remove.

Removes the directory from the current drive. You will need to remove all of the files from the directory before it can be deleted (*see* DELETE, "Deleting Document Files").

DISPLAY SETTINGS

1. Choose File, Preferences, Display.
2. Choose the settings you want to turn on or off, or change.
3. Choose OK when done.
4. Choose Close.

Changes the way various WordPerfect features are displayed in the window. Items that can be displayed or turned off are document name, symbols such as paragraph, space, and tab marks, View/Zoom, Reveal Codes, Ruler, Merge, table cell guides, system colors, comments, graphics, hidden text, and the scroll bars. You can also change the way measurements are displayed. Choices of measurements are in inches either with the (") or with an (i), centimeters, millimeters, points, or 1200th of an inch. Inches (") is the default.

DOCUMENT COMPARE

Adding Markings

1. Open a document you want to compare, and edit it. Add or delete text or make any other changes.
2. Choose File, Compare Document.
3. Choose Add Markings.
4. Select the type of comparison: Word (the default), Phrase, Sentence, or Paragraph.
5. Choose OK or press ENTER.
6. Choose Yes.

Compares the edited open document with the version of the same document that is saved on disk; or you can enter the name of a different document, if you like. The name of the document that is to be used for the comparison is displayed in the Compare Current

Document to: text box. Type a different filename here, or click the button at the end of the text box to go to the Select File dialog box where you can select a filename. Choose OK or press ENTER when done.

The types of comparisons determine how the text is marked. Choose Word to mark each word that is different; choose Phrase to mark groups of words that are different; choose Sentence to mark entire sentences; and Paragraph to mark entire paragraphs that are different.

Text that is deleted from the first version is shown as "strikeout" text. New text that is not in the first version is shown as "redlined" (red color) text.

Removing Markings

1. Choose File, Compare Document, Remove Markings.
2. Choose either Remove Redline Markings and Strikeout Text, or Remove Strikeout Text Only.
3. Choose OK or press ENTER.

Removes the comparison markings and restores the document to the way it was before you compared it to another document. Depending upon the use of your document, you may want to keep the redlining as an indication of new text that has been added. Frequently when several people are involved in producing a document, it is helpful to mark added edits.

DOCUMENT INFO

1. Open a document.
2. Choose File, Document Info to display the Document Information box.
3. Choose Cancel to remove it from the window.

Displays a list of items providing information about the current document. This list includes number of characters, words, lines, sentences, paragraphs, and pages. It also shows the average length of words and sentences and the maximum words per sentence.

DOCUMENT SUMMARY

Creating a Document Summary

1. Choose File, Document Summary.
2. Enter appropriate information in the text boxes. You can click the scroll bar to see additional fields.
3. Choose OK when done.

Provides summary information about the document such as creation date, revision date, title, description of contents, author, typist, subject, account, keywords, and abstract. The summary is not printed as part of the document unless you choose to do that in the Options dialog box.

You can choose Options in the Document Summary dialog box to print the summary, delete it from the document, extract information from the document (which copies some document information and places it automatically in some of the summary fields), save the summary as a new document. (*See also* PRINT.)

Adding or Deleting Fields in the Document Summary

1. Choose File, Document Summary, Configure.
2. The Selected Fields currently in use are shown in the list box at the left in the dialog box.
3. Choose Available Fields.
4. Select any additional fields from the list; select any fields that are currently included (they show an X in the box) to remove them from the list of selected fields; or choose Clear All to remove all field names from the list of selected fields.
5. Choose OK or press ENTER.

6. Choose OK or press ENTER again to return to the document.

Customizes the Document Summary dialog box and allows you to add or remove information, depending upon your work. When a field is added to the document summary, it is placed automatically at the end of the list. You can drag it to a different position in the list, if you like. To make the change the default, choose Use As Default and choose Yes.

Changing Summary Preferences

1. Choose File, Preferences, Summary.
2. Make changes to any of the options.
3. Choose OK.
4. Choose Close.

The options that can be changed are listed in the following table:

Options	Results
Default Subject Text	Specify a default word that will automatically enter information. For example, the default subject is RE:, which means that in a memo, the text following the RE: will be inserted automatically as the subject in the summary. You can enter any word that you want here, and the text following it will be inserted as the subject.
Default Descriptive Type	Enter a description here if all documents are the same type. For example, if your documents are always memos, enter **Memo** here to describe the document.
Use Descriptive Names	Turn this on to always show the descriptive name in the Document Summary dialog box.
Create Summary on Save/Exit	Turn this on to always show the Summary dialog box when saving a document.

Specifies the summary features that will be the defaults for all subsequent WordPerfect documents.

DOS, GO TO

1. Hold down the ALT key and press TAB until you see the Program Manager box. Release the keys.
2. Open the Main group icon if it is not already open.
3. Double-click the MS-DOS Prompt icon to go to DOS.
4. To return to Windows, type **exit** at the prompt C:\WINDOWS> and press ENTER.
5. Press ALT+TAB until the WP document box is displayed, and release the keys to return to the WordPerfect document.

Goes out to the DOS prompt where you can enter DOS commands.

DOUBLE INDENT

See INDENT

DOUBLE-UNDERLINE

Keyboard

1. Move the insertion point to the position where double-underlining is to begin.
2. Choose Layout, Font. (Or press F9.)
3. Choose Double-Underline.
4. Choose OK or press ENTER.
5. Type the text.
6. Choose Layout, Font, Double-Underline, then OK or ENTER to end the formatting.

Mouse

1. Move the insertion point to the position where double-underlining is to begin.
2. Click the right mouse button and choose Font. Then follow the preceding steps 3 through 6.

Formats characters with a double-underline. Spaces are underlined by default. To turn off underlining spaces, select Spaces (tab to it—a border will be around it when it is selected), and press Enter to remove the X. Repeat this to turn it back on. There is no hot key to select Spaces. To turn on or off underlining tabs, choose Tabs.

Note *To add double-underlining to existing text, select the text and then follow the previous steps to apply formatting.*

DRAFT VIEW

1. Choose View, Draft. (Or press CTRL+F5.)

Shows the document with font attributes displayed as they will be printed. Bold, italic, underlining, and so on will appear on the screen as they will be printed; however, headers and footers, watermarks, margins, and some other formatting are not shown. Draft view is faster than other views because some formatting is not displayed; for example, page breaks will use less space.

Note *To leave Draft view, Choose View, Page (ALT+F5) or Two-Page.*

DRAG AND DROP

Drag and drop is a function that can only be used with the mouse.

1. Select the text to be moved.
2. Point to the selection and hold down the left mouse button. A rectangle is added to the arrow.

3. To move the selection, drag to a new location and release the left mouse button.
4. To copy the selection, press the CTRL key and drag to a new location.
5. Click at any position outside the selection to turn off the highlighting.

Moves or copies selected text to a new position in the document. You cannot move the selection into areas in the window where text or hard returns have not been entered.

DRAW

Keyboard

1. Choose Graphics, Draw.
2. Create a drawing.
3. Choose File, Exit and Return to Document when done.
4. Choose Yes to save changes and insert the drawing in the WordPerfect document.

Mouse

1. Click the Draw button in the Button Bar.
2. Create a drawing.
3. Double-click the Control-menu box at the left end of the WP Draw title bar.
4. Choose Yes to save changes and insert the drawing in the WordPerfect document

Goes to the WP Draw window, where you can create drawings and text using the Draw palette and options.

Note *To edit a drawing, double-click it in the document window. (You will return to the WP Draw window where you can make changes.) Use the previous steps to return to the document. If you are using the keyboard, choose Graphics, Edit Box (or press SHIFT+F11), choose the box* *number that you want to edit and press ENTER, then choose Edit, Activate WP Graphic 2.1 Object.*

ENDNOTES

Creating an Endnote

1. Move the insertion point to the position where you want to insert the endnote.
2. Choose Insert, Endnote, Create. The Endnote features bar is displayed.
3. Type text for the endnote.
4. Choose Close to return to the document.

Inserts an endnote number at the insertion point. The text of the endnote is placed at the end of the document.

The Endnote features bar also provides you with the opportunity to view the next or previous endnotes in your document, or to insert a note number in the endnote text.

Note *Press ALT+SHIFT and the underlined character to choose an item in the Endnote features bar if you are using the keyboard.*

Editing an Endnote

1. Choose Insert, Endnote, Edit.
2. Type the endnote number in the Endnote Number text box.
3. Choose OK or press ENTER.
4. Make the changes in the endnote text.
5. Choose Close.

Moves the insertion point to the endnote text where edits can be made. You can also manually move the insertion point to the endnote text and edit it.

Using Endnote Options

1. Move the insertion point to the place where you want the changes to begin.
2. Choose Insert, Endnote, Options and make any changes to the options (see the following list).
3. Choose OK when done.

Changes the endnote options from the insertion point to the end of the document, or until you make additional changes. You can choose from any of the following options:

- *Method* selects the numbering method. You can choose upper- or lowercase letters; or upper- or lowercase roman numerals.
- *Characters* selects the character you can use in place of a number for the endnote.
- *In Text* edits the numbering style of the reference number that is inserted in the text; *In Note* changes the number in the endnote.
- *Space* changes the spacing between notes. Enter a measurement that you want. The default is 1/6 inch or 1 line.
- *Amount of Endnote to Keep Together* specifies the amount of space for the endnote. The default is 1/2 inch. Enter a measurement that you want.

Changes the endnote options from the insertion point to the end of the document, or until you make additional changes.

Changing Endnote Placement

Endnote numbers are placed by default at the insertion point and are numbered consecutively throughout the document. If you want to restart the numbering at 1 on each page, choose Insert, Endnote, Placement and turn on Insert Endnotes at Insertion Point and Restart Numbering.

ENVELOPES

Keyboard

1. Choose Layout, Envelope.

   Note *If a paper definition for an envelope has not been created previously, you will be prompted to do that. Respond to the dialog boxes that are displayed. When you are done the Envelope dialog box will be displayed and you can proceed with the following steps.*

2. Type the return address in the Return Addresses text box.
3. Type the mailing address in the Mailing Addresses text box.
4. If you use an envelope that is a different size from the default, choose Envelope Definitions and select a new envelope size.
5. Choose Print Envelope. Be sure your printer is on-line and an envelope is inserted in the appropriate bin.

Mouse

1. Click the Envelope button in the Button Bar. Then follow the preceding steps 2 through 5.

Prints an envelope using the default settings. The Add options for the return address and mailing address are used to store frequently used addresses. Type the return addresses that you want to use and choose Add; type the mailing addresses and choose Add. Repeat these steps for additional addresses. The next time you use the envelope feature, these addresses will be displayed in the return address and mailing address list boxes (located just below the address text boxes) and can be selected and used in the current envelope.

You can choose Options in the Envelope dialog box to change the position of the return and mailing addresses and to include a bar code. You can also choose Append to Doc to add the envelope at the end of the current document. (*See also* BAR CODES.)

Choose Create New Definition if you are using an envelope that is not available in the envelope definition list. Enter a name for the definition, enter the appropriate paper type and size, select the orientation, and make other adjustments as needed. Choose OK. The new definition is now added to the list of envelope definitions.

ENVIRONMENT

1. Choose File, Preferences, Environment.
2. Make changes that you want.
3. Choose OK when done.
4. Choose Close.

Makes changes in the way WordPerfect responds in the general working environment. The following changes can be made: display user information; set beeps on errors, hyphenation, or search failure; set the hyphenation prompt, designate whether or not to confirm deletions, change menu displays, specify when to save the workspace, and set save options.

EQUATIONS

Creating an Equation

1. Move the insertion point to the place where you want to insert an equation.
2. Choose Graphics, Equation.
3. Enter the equation in the editing pane (the top one-third of the window). See the example later in this section.
4. Choose View, Redisplay; click on the Redisplay button in the Button Bar in the Equation Editor window; or press CTRL+F3.

5. Choose File, Close; click the Close button in the Button Bar in the Equation Editor window; or press CTRL+F4.

Inserts an equation that is automatically set up in the correct format depending upon the commands that have been entered in the editing pane. The equation cannot be used to perform calculations. The Equation Editor is only used to set up equations easily and accurately.

To enter the equation in the editing pane, type the numbers or letters in the equation almost as you would say them, and double-click the commands in the list at the left of the Equation Editor window to insert them in the editing pane. For example, to create a formula to find an interest rate, you might say to yourself, "Rate equals Interest divided by (Principal times Time)." Type **R = I** then double-click OVER in the command list, double-click the left curly bracket ({), type **P X T**, and double-click the right curly bracket (}). After entering the text in the editing pane, press CTRL+F3 to redisplay.

If you want to save frequently used equations as separate files in the Equation Editor, choose File, Save As (F3). They can then be inserted later in the Equation Editor window by choosing File, Insert File (F4), Retrieve, and pressing Ctrl+F3 to redisplay. The formatted equation can then be inserted in the document. You can also insert the text for the equation directly into the document window by choosing Insert, File; however, when you do this, only the text is displayed—it is not formatted as an equation.

The edit functions in the Equation Editor are similar to those in a WordPerfect document window. You can use Zoom, change fonts, insert characters, record and run macros, or turn the Equation Palette and Button Bar off and on. The document initial font is used for the equation, but you can change this the same way you change fonts in the document window.

Using Commands and Symbols

Commands are displayed as the default in the Equation Palette at the left of the Equation Editor window. As you select each command, the syntax is displayed in the status bar. You can change the list displayed in the Equation Palette by clicking on the button at the top of the Palette text box—a pop-up list is displayed. Choose an item from the list, and the symbols or commands in that group will then be displayed in the Palette.

To insert a command or symbol, double-click it; or select the command and press ENTER if you are using the keyboard. In some groups, you can choose to insert either the keyword or the symbol that represents it. To do this, select the command and click either Keyword or Symbol.

EXIT

Keyboard

1. Choose File, Exit. (Or press ALT+F4.)

Mouse

1. Double-click the Control-menu box at the left end of the title bar.

Exits from the WordPerfect window and returns to Windows. You will be prompted to name any unnamed documents, or to save any edits to documents that have been named previously. The system will display each document in turn and give you the opportunity to save or not save each.

FIND

1. Choose Edit, Find. (Or press F2.)
2. Type the text that you want to locate in the Find text box.
3. Choose Find Next.

Searches for and locates text that matches the text entered in the Find text box. You can also tailor the search to meet specific conditions. You can choose from any of the following options:

- *Type, Specific Codes* locates codes for fonts, justification, margins, line spacing, styles, overstrike, and so on.
- *Match* specifies whether to search for Whole Word, Case, Font, or Codes.
- *Action* specifies what happens when the item is located. The options here include Select Match, which will select the item that is located; Position Before and Position After, which control the location of the insertion point when the item is located; and Extend Selection, which extends the selection from the current insertion point to the item that is located.
- *Options* allows you to control where the search will look in the current document. The search can begin at the top of the document; it can be only within a selection; or at the end of the search, it can wrap back to the beginning of the document. Searching in headers and footers is the default, but this can be turned off here.
- *Find Next or Find Prev* looks for the next or previous occurrence of the same text or codes. The Find Text dialog box remains on the screen until you choose Close to remove it.

FLUSH RIGHT

Aligning One Line of Text at the Right Margin

1. Move the insertion point to the place where you want to begin flush right alignment.
2. Choose Layout, Line, Flush Right. (Or press ALT+F7.)
3. Type the text.

4. Press ENTER to end the alignment and return to Left Flush.

Aligns the line of text at the right margin. This is used to enter text such as report, account, or product numbers at the right margin; or enter any other text that you want to align there.

Note *You also can apply Flush Right to text that has been typed previously or select existing text with a different alignment. Just move the insertion point to the beginning of the line and press ALT+F7.*

Using Right Justification

Keyboard

1. Move the insertion point to the place where you want to begin formatting with right justification.
2. Choose Layout, Justification, Right. (Or press CTRL+R.)

Mouse

1. Move the insertion point to the place where you want to begin formatting with right justification.
2. Click on the Justification button in the Power Bar and drag to choose Right.

Aligns all lines of text at the right margin. If you press ENTER to go to the next line, right justification will continue. All lines will be right aligned until you end the formatting. To end right justification, press CTRL+L to return to left alignment (or press any other shortcut keys to go to a different type of alignment) or click on the Justification button and select a different alignment.

Note *You can also apply Right Justification to a selected block of text using these same steps.*

FONTS

Choosing a Font Face, Style, and Size

Keyboard

1. Move the insertion point to the place where you want to begin using a different font.
2. Choose Layout, Font to go to the Font dialog box. (Or press F9.)
3. Choose a Font Face from the list box.
4. Choose a Font Style from the list in the Font Style list box. The choices displayed depend on the font face that was chosen.
5. Choose a Font Size from the list.
6. Choose OK when done.

Mouse

1. Move the insertion point to the place where you want to begin using a different font.
2. Click on the Font Face button in the Power Bar and choose a Font from the drop-down list.
3. Click on the Font Size button in the Power Bar, and choose a size from the drop-down list.

Formats text with the font from the insertion point on, until you use these same steps to select a different font.

- *Font Face* refers to the name of the font, such as Courier, Times Roman, Helvetica, and so on. It is the general outline of the way all the characters are formed for that face regardless of size or style.
- *Font Style* refers to different appearances of the general outline. The styles available depend upon the face that was selected—regular, italic, bold, bold italic, and so on.
- *Font Size* refers to the size of the characters. It is selected on the basis of the point size, which reflects the height of

the characters. If a character is 12 points, it means that you can type 6 lines to an inch. There are 72 points per inch; therefore 12 is 1/6th of an inch. A font that is 30 points is almost 1/2 inch high.

An example of your choices is shown in the Resulting font box in the Font dialog box, allowing you to see your choice before returning to the document. You can also see an example of formatting at the right end of the status bar when you return to the document window.

Changing the Appearance of Text

The appearance of text can be changed by adding characteristics such as bold, underline, double-underline, italic, shadow, strikeout and so on. Ten appearance characteristics are available for formatting and are included in the Font dialog box. Some of the font faces also include bold and italic as font styles. In those cases, you can just select the font style and not turn on the corresponding appearance characterstics.

Keyboard

1. Move the insertion point to the place where you want to format the characters with a different appearance.
2. Choose Layout, Font. (Or press F9.)
3. Click on the appearance characteristic or press ALT and the underlined letter of the characteristic you want. The Resulting Font box shows how the characters will look.
4. Choose OK or press ENTER.

Mouse

1. Move the insertion point to the place where you want to format the characters with a different appearance.
2. Click on the Bold Font, Italic Font, or Underline Font button in the Power Bar. The button is depressed when the formatting is turned on. Click on the buttons to end the formatting, as well. The button will no longer be depressed.

Note *You can also click on the right mouse button, choose Font, select other characteristics in the Font dialog box, and choose OK.*

Formats the characters from the insertion point on with a different appearance characteristic. To format text as Hidden, first turn on Hidden Text in the View menu. Follow these same steps to turn off the appearance characteristics.

Note *Appearance characteristics can be applied to text after it is typed by selecting the text and using the steps just given to change the appearance.*

Using Document Initial Font

1. Choose Layout, Font. (Or press F9.)
2. Choose Initial Font to go to the Document Initial Font dialog box.
3. Select the Font Face, Size, and Style from the lists.
4. Choose OK to return to the Font dialog box and then choose OK again to return to the document.

Selects a font that will be applied to the entire document regardless of where your insertion point is located when you do this. The font will be saved with the current document, but will not change other documents. You can still use different fonts within the document for portions of the text.

Note *You can also choose Layout, Document, Initial Font to make this change. The Font Map option in the Font dialog box lets you designate the font that will be used for an automatic font change if the one you selected is not available.*

FOOTERS

See HEADERS/FOOTERS

FOOTNOTES

Creating a Footnote

1. Move the insertion point to the place where you want to insert a footnote number.
2. Choose Insert, Footnote, Create.
3. Type the text for the footnote.
4. Choose Close from the Footnote features bar to return to the document window.

Inserts a footnote number at the insertion point in the text. The footnote text is displayed at the bottom of the page below a separator line.

Editing a Footnote

1. Choose Insert, Footnote, Edit.
2. Enter the number that you want in the Footnote Number text box.
3. Choose OK or press ENTER.
4. Edit the footnote text.
5. Choose Close from the Footnote features bar to return to the document window.

Displays the Footnote features bar and allows you to edit the footnote text. Footnotes are displayed in Page view and in Two-Page view; however, they are not displayed in Draft view.

Note *If you are using a mouse and are working in Page or in Two-Page view, you can click on the footnote text and edit it without using the steps given above.*

Using Footnote Options

1. Choose Insert, Footnote, Options.
2. Make changes in the Footnote Options dialog box. (See the following bulleted list.)
3. Choose OK or press ENTER.

Allows you to make any of the following changes:

- *Method* selects the numbering method. The default is to use numbers; however, you can choose upper- or lowercase letters, upper- or lowercase Roman numerals, or you can enter a different character.
- *In Text* edits the numbering style of the reference number that is inserted in the text; *In Note* changes the number in the footnote.
- *Space* changes the spacing between notes. Enter a measurement or click buttons to change the value.
- *Place Notes at Bottom of Page* specifies the default position of the note. The other choice here is *Place Notes Below Text* which will display the footnote text below the paragraph containing the footnote number.
- *Amount of Footnote to Keep Together* specifies the amount of space for the footnote. The default amount is 1/2 inch. You can enter the amount or click on the incrementing (arrow) button to select a different amount.
- *Insert (Continued) Message* displays the word "Continued" where a footnote cannot fit on the current page. The default is for this to be turned off.
- *Separator* displays the Line Separator dialog box. By default a line is inserted between the text and the footnote area. You can turn this off in the Line Separator dialog box by choosing None as the Line Style; or you can choose a different line style. You can also change the spacing above and below the separator line, choose a different Line Position, or specify a Length of Line.

GENERATE

See INDEX, TABLE OF AUTHORITIES, TABLE OF CONTENTS, and CROSS-REFERENCE

GO TO

Going to a Specific Page

Keyboard

1. Choose Edit, Go To. (Or press CTRL+G.)
2. Enter the page number or select it from the list.
3. Choose OK or press ENTER.

Moves the insertion point quickly to the top of the specified page.

Mouse

1. To go to the next page or previous page, click on the up or down page buttons at the bottom of the vertical scroll bar.

Other options in the Go To dialog box are

- *Position* selects a position on the page to go to—Last, Top, or Bottom.
- *Bookmark* allows you to enter the bookmark name or select from a list.
- *Table* allows you to choose from the list. You can also specify a cell within the table by typing the cell address in the Cell/Range text box or selecting from a list.

GRAMMAR

Keyboard

1. Choose Tools, Grammatik. (Or press ALT+SHIFT+F1.)
2. Choose Start. A suggestion is displayed at the first error. Or if the first error is a spelling error, the spelling dialog box is displayed and you can make the correction.
3. Choose Replace to replace with the suggested change. Or if several words are displayed for the correction, select the one you want and then choose Replace.

You can also choose Ignore Word to go on without changing, or choose Next Sentence. Add allows you to add words to the Grammatik dictionary.

4. Repeat step 3 at subsequent errors or suggestions. A check box below the menu bar indicates the type of problem.
5. Choose Close when done.

Mouse

1. Click on the Grammatik button in the Power Bar. Then follow the preceding steps 2 through 5.

Checks sentences for errors in grammar and spelling. The grammar checker also identifies sentences written in passive voice and displays a suggestion for active voice. Choose any of the following to control the way text is checked:

- *Check* specifies the text to be checked: Sentence, Paragraph, Document (the default), To End of Document, or Selected Text.
- *Options* selects Writing Style from the list of predefined styles and specifies the following Checking Options: paragraph errors, ignore periods in words, and suggest spelling replacements. It also specifies the rule classes that control the grammar check. The rule classes are Grammar, Mechanics, and Styles, or only Grammar and Mechanics. *Grammar* checks parts of speech and usage. *Mechanics* checks capitalization, punctuation, and spelling. *Style* indicates passive voice, jargon, cliches, and wordiness. Choose Statistics to display a count of words, syllables, sentences, paragraphs, and so on.

Changes the way items are checked. If there are some features that you never use, turn them off. It will probably speed up the grammar check.

GRAPHICS

See also CHART, DRAW, EQUATION, and TEXTART

Inserting a Figure

Keyboard

1. Move the insertion point to the place where you want to insert a figure.
2. Choose Graphics, Figure.
3. Choose the name of the figure file from the Filename list.
4. Choose View if you want to see the figure before inserting it in the document.
5. Choose OK or press ENTER.

Mouse

1. Move the insertion point to the place where you want to insert a figure.
2. Click on the Figure button in the Button Bar. Then follow the preceding steps 3 through 5.

Inserts a WordPerfect supplied figure in the current document, and the feature bar is displayed so that you can edit the figure if you like. (*See* "Editing a Box," later in this section.) Figure filenames end with the extension .WPG. The default style for a figure box includes a single line border on all sides, paragraph anchor type, horizontal placement at the right margin, automatic height, and width set at 3.25 inches. (*See* "Editing Graphic Styles" later in this section for information on changing the style.)

Inserting a Text Box

Keyboard

1. Move the insertion point to the place where you want to insert a text box.
2. Choose Graphics, Text.

Mouse

1. Move the insertion point to the place where you want to insert a text box.
2. Click on the Text Box button in the Button Bar.

Inserts a text box at the insertion point and displays the feature bar. Type any text in the box and format it the way you want. You can also make changes in the text box using the feature bar. (*See* "Editing a Box.")

To return the insertion point to the regular document text, click at any position outside the text box or choose Close from the feature bar.

Creating Equations

See EQUATIONS

Using a Custom Box

1. Move the insertion point to the place where you want to insert the box.
2. Choose Graphics, Custom Box.
3. Select a Style Name from the list at the left in the Custom Box dialog box. The example box at the right of the Style Name list displays the border style for the selection.
4. Other features of the selected box styles—Box Placement, Content, Height, Horizontal and Vertical Position, and Width—are displayed at the bottom of the dialog box.
5. If you like, you can change the box style before inserting it by choosing Styles, Edit. Then change the caption, position, size, and so on.
6. Choose OK.

Inserts a custom box at the insertion point and displays the Graphic feature bar, which can be used to change the box. (*See* "Editing a Box" for information on changing the styles.)

Editing a Box

1. Choose Graphics, Edit Box. (Or press SHIFT+F11.)
2. Choose the Document Box Number that you want to edit. (If only one box is in the document, the feature bar will be displayed immediately.)
3. Choose OK or press ENTER.
4. Use the feature bar to make changes.
5. Choose Close when done.

Displays the feature bar and allows you to choose items that you want to change in the selected graphic box. The changes affect only the selected box; however, similar changes can be made to a graphic style (*see* "Editing Graphic Styles" in this section). Options in the feature bar and changes that you can make are as follows:

- *Caption* displays the Box Caption dialog box. Choose Edit to insert a caption number and move the insertion point to the caption area where you can type the text for the caption. Make other changes in the Box Caption dialog box, such as position, width, and so on.
- *Content* displays the Box Content dialog box. Choose Edit to move the insertion point into the box and make any changes there or if you are editing a draw figure you will go to the Draw window. Other changes you can make depend upon the type of box.
- *Position* sets the position of the box on the page and specifies the anchor type. Page Anchor places the box at a fixed position on the page. Paragraph Anchor places the box in the current paragraph, where it can be moved up or down in the document as text is inserted or deleted above the paragraph. Character Anchor allows the box to move left or right or up or down, the same way characters move in a document.
- *Size* sets the height and width of the box. Or you can leave height and width at Size to Content, which makes the box fit the size of the contents in it.
- *Border/Fill* sets a border and fill style for the box. Choose Off to remove the current borders. You can click on the

Border Style and Fill Style buttons to display and select the styles you want. Choose Customize Style to customize each side separately, if you like.

- *Wrap* selects the method for wrapping document text around the box. Examples are shown for each method.
- *Style* selects the box style you want. This changes the style of box; and the default settings of the new box style, such as borders, paragraph position, caption position, and so on, will be applied automatically.
- *Tools* displays a palette that provides options for editing an image. This is not available when editing a text box.
- *Next or Prev* goes to the next or previous graphic box.
- *Close* removes the feature bar from the window.

Editing Graphic Styles

1. Move the insertion point to where you want the style changes to take effect.
2. Choose Graphics, Graphics Styles.
3. Select a type of box from Styles list.
4. Choose Edit.
5. Make changes that you want to Caption, Content, Position, and so on.
6. Choose OK or press ENTER.
7. Choose Close.

Changes the characteristics of the graphic style from the insertion point on. All boxes of the type that you select will display the changes that were made to the style. The choices in the Edit Box Style dialog box are similar to those in the Graphics feature bar.

Inserting a Horizontal Line

1. Move the insertion point to the place where you want to insert a line.
2. Choose Graphics, Horizontal Line. (Or press CTRL+F11.)

Inserts a horizontal line at the insertion point. The default line extends from the left margin to the right margin;

however, this can be changed. *See* "Editing Lines" for information on changing lines.

Inserting a Vertical Line

1. Move the insertion point to the place where you want to insert the vertical line.
2. Choose Graphics, Vertical line. (Or press CTRL+SHIFT+F11.)

Inserts a vertical line at the left margin that extends the full length of the page. *See* "Editing Lines" (next) for changing the lines.

Editing Lines

1. Move the insertion point directly in front of the code for the line you want to change.
2. Choose Graphics, Edit Line.
3. Make changes in the dialog box.
4. Choose OK or press ENTER.

Edits the current line. If you choose Graphics, Custom Line and make changes, they will be in effect from the insertion point on.

Changes that can be made in the Edit Graphic Line dialog box are as follows:

- *Line Style* selects the style from a list. An example is displayed in the example box.
- *Horizontal or Vertical* selects the line type to be edited.
- *Position—Horizontal or Vertical*—specifies a placement on the page.
- *Length* sets the length of the line.
- *Spacing: Above Line* and *Below Line* designates the amount of space between the line and adjacent text.
- *Line Color* selects a color if you have a color printer.
- *Thickness* designates the width of the line.

Changes the line currently displayed in the document. You can also choose Line Styles in the Edit Graphics Line dialog box, select a line style to be edited, choose Edit or Create, make changes in the Edit Line Style dialog box, and choose OK when done. These changes will be permanent. If you choose to create a new line style, it will be added to the list of Line Styles.

Using the Mouse to Edit a Graphic

1. Double-click on the graphic.
2. Make changes.
3. Click anywhere outside the box to leave it. Choose OK if a dialog box is displayed, or if you are in the Draw or Mini-Makeup Window, double-click on the Control-menu box at the left end of the title bar to exit from a window.

Allows you to edit depending on the type of box. If you double-click on a figure, drawing, or chart you will go to the appropriate WordPerfect window to make the changes. If you double-click on a text box, the insertion point will move into the box where you can make edits. Double-click on a line to display the Edit Graphics Line dialog box.

Using the Mouse to Move a Box or Line

1. Click on the box or line to display the four-sided arrow.
2. Hold down the left mouse button, drag the outline to a different position, and release.
3. Click outside the box or line to remove the handles.

Moves the box or line to a different position.

Using the Mouse to Change the Size of a Box or Line

1. Click on the box or line to display the four-sided arrow.
2. Point to one of the handles. The pointer becomes a two-sided arrow.

3. Hold down the left mouse button, drag the side or corner to change the size of the box or line, and release the button.
4. Click outside the box or line to remove the handles.

Changes the size of the box or line. You can change each side separately or you can drag a corner, which will change the two adjacent sides.

HARD SPACE

1. Move the insertion point to the place where you want to insert a hard space.
2. Choose Layout, Line, Other Codes. (Or press CTRL+SPACEBAR.)
3. Choose Hard Space to turn it on.
4. Choose Insert.

Inserts a hard space code [HSpace] at the insertion point. Hard spaces are used to keep words together on the same line. For example, insert a hard space in place of a normal space between a title and a name, between months and days and years, or city and states in addresses to keep these items on the same line.

HEADERS/FOOTERS

1. Move the insertion point to the first page where you want the headers or footers to begin.
2. Choose Layout, Header/Footer.
3. Select the type of first or second header or footer.
4. Choose Create.
5. Type the text for the header or footer.
6. Choose Close from the feature bar or click anywhere in the document if you are in Page view.

Note *The default placement of headers and footers is in the text page, not in the margins; therefore, if you create your document without a header and footer and choose to add them later, your page endings may be changed.*

Places a header or footer in the document. If you are in Page view, the header or footer will be displayed in the text. If you are in Draft view, the headers and footers will not be showing.

You can select four different types of headers or footers. Header text appears at the top of pages; footer text appears at the bottom of pages from the insertion point on, or until you choose Discontinue.

You can insert two headers (A and B) and two footers (A and B) if you like. This allows you to display different header or footer text on alternating pages. For example, you may want a chapter name and number in a header on a left facing page and a topic in the header on the right facing page. To do this, choose Placement from the Header/Footer feature bar and select the type of placement you want for each header of footer.

Editing Headers/Footers

1. Choose Layout, Header/Footer.
2. Select the header or footer to be edited.
3. Choose Edit.
4. Make the changes to the text or use the feature bar to make other changes. See list below.
5. Choose Close to remove the feature bar, or click in the document if you are in Page view.

Allows you to edit the text of the header or footer or to make other changes. The features that can be changed are as follows:

- *Number* from the Header/Footer feature bar selects a type of number—Page, Secondary, Chapter or Volume—that is inserted in the header or footer.
- *Line* inserts a graphic line in the header or footer.

- *Placement* selects Odd pages, Even pages, or Every page.
- *Distance* sets a distance between the text and the header or footer.
- *Next or Previous* goes to the next or the previous header or footer.

Discontinuing a Header or Footer

1. Move the insertion point to the page where you want to end the header or footer.
2. Choose Layout, Header/Footer.
3. Select the header or footer type.
4. Choose Discontinue.

Turns off the header or footer from that page on in the active document. Repeat these steps for each header or footer that you want to discontinue.

HELP

1. Choose Help.
2. Select one of the following: Contents, Search for Help On, How Do I, Macros, Coach, Tutorial, and About WordPerfect.

Shortcut Keys

1. Move the insertion point to the area about which you want Help information.
2. Press F1 to display context-sensitive information.

Accesses the WordPerfect help function.

HIDDEN TEXT

See FONT, "Changing the Appearance of Text"

HIDE BARS

1. Choose View, Hide Bars. (Or press ALT+SHIFT+F5.)
2. Choose OK.

Removes the menu, Ruler Bar, Power Bar, Button Bar, status bar, and scroll bars from the screen. The Hide Bars Information dialog box is displayed when this item is chosen. You can display more document text if you remove these features from the screen.

Note *To restore these features, press the* ESC *key, or press* ALT+V *to display the View menu, and choose Hide Bars.*

HYPERTEXT

Creating a Hypertext Link

1. Select Tools, Hypertext to display the feature bar.
2. Choose Create.
3. Enter the name of the bookmark or choose from the Go To Bookmark list. Or choose Go To Other Document, enter the document name or select one from the list, and then select a bookmark name in that document.
4. Choose OK or press ENTER. The status bar now shows a different color font as the example for the hypertext reference.
5. Enter text that indicates the reference to the bookmark or other appropriate text, if you like. It is displayed in a format different from the rest of the document text.
6. Choose Close to remove the feature bar.

Creates a link that allows you to go quickly from the hypertext link to the bookmark. This is generally intended for online use and is helpful when you want to refer to information in other parts of the active document, or in other documents. After using the link, you can delete it, and the text is then formatted in normal characters.

Using the Hypertext Link

Keyboard

1. Choose Tools, Hypertext to display the feature bar.
2. Move the insertion point to the hypertext, as indicated by the different formatting.
3. Choose Perform to jump to the linked bookmark.
4. Choose Back to return to the hypertext.

Mouse

1. To jump to the linked bookmark, click on the hypertext when Deactivate is showing in the feature bar. When Deactivate is showing, it means the link is activated, allowing you to click on hypertext to jump (Deactivate is the other choice, at this point). If Activate is showing, it means the link is deactivated, and you should choose Perform to jump to the linked bookmark.

Jumps quickly to the bookmark.

Other options in the feature bar are:

- *Next* goes to the next hypertext link in the active document.
- *Previous* goes to the previous link in the active document.
- *Create* creates another link.
- *Edit* changes the bookmark name that is linked to the current hypertext. You can select a different bookmark name, if you like.
- *Delete* removes the link and returns the text to the same as other text in the document.
- *Style* changes the formatting characteristics used for the hypertext characters.

See also BOOKMARK.

HYPHENATION

1. Move the insertion point to the place where you want to begin hyphenation.
2. Choose Layout, Line, Hyphenation.
3. Turn Hyphenation On. An X should be showing in the box.
4. Choose OK or press ENTER.

Inserts a hyphenation code [Hyph] in the text. From that point on, words that are in the hyphenation zone will be hyphenated, or you will be prompted to hyphenate words if they do not exist in the dictionary.

If you are inserting the code in a document that already contains text, hyphens will be inserted automatically as needed, or you will be prompted to place them until the end of the document is reached. If the hyphenation code is inserted as text is typed, the prompts will be displayed or hyphens will be inserted automatically, as needed.

The default hyphenation prompt, set in the Environment Preferences dialog box, is to prompt only When Required—*required* meaning the word does not appear in the dictionary, and you will be prompted to place the hyphen. When you are prompted to hyphenate a word, the word is displayed in a text box. Press the arrow keys to move the hyphen to the position where you want to insert it and choose Insert Hyphen.

Note *The hyphenation zone is an area at the right margin that determines whether or not a word is hyphenated. If the word is longer than the hyphenation zone, it will be divided when hyphenation is turned on. The size of this area is a percentage of the line length and can be changed in the Line Hyphenation dialog box. Percent Left refers to the percentage of the line that is to the left of the right margin. Percent Right is the percentage that is to the right of the right margin.*

Setting Default Hyphenation

1. Choose File, Preferences, Environment.
2. Make changes to the default hyphenation prompts.
3. Choose OK or press ENTER.
4. Choose Close.

Changes the hyphenation settings permanently.

The changes that can be made are

- *Hyphenation Prompt* can be set to Always, Never, or When Required.
- *Beep* can be set to on or off for Hyphenation. When beep is on, which is the default, an X is shown in the check box.

Inserting a Hyphen Code in Text

1. Move the insertion point to the place where you want to insert the hyphen.
2. Choose Layout, Line, Other Codes. (Or press the hyphen (-) key.)
3. Choose Hyphen.
4. Choose Insert.

Connects words with a hyphen. If the words cross the hyphenation zone, they will break at the hyphen.

Inserting a Hyphen Character in Text

1. Move the insertion point to the place where you want to insert the hyphen character.
2. Choose Layout, Line, Other Codes. (Or press CTRL+-.)
3. Choose Hyphen Character.
4. Choose Insert.

Keeps hyphenated words together on the same line. No code is inserted, only a hyphen character (-) will be displayed in Reveal Codes.

Inserting a Soft Hyphen in Text

1. Move the insertion point to the place where you want to insert the soft hyphen.
2. Choose Layout, Line, Other Codes. (Or press CTRL+SHIFT+-.)
3. Choose Soft Hyphen to turn it on.
4. Choose Insert.

Inserts a soft hyphen code [-Soft Hyphen] in a word. The hyphen will only divide the word when it is positioned in the hyphenation zone at the right margin. The hyphen will not show if the word is not divided.

Inserting a Hyphenation Soft Return

1. Move the insertion point to the place where you want to insert the hyphenation soft return.
2. Choose Layout, Line, Other Codes.
3. Choose Hyphenation Soft Return to turn it on.
4. Choose Insert.

Inserts a hyphenation soft return code [Hyph SRt] in the text. This code is used to divide a word at the right margin without inserting a hyphen. The first part of the word is on the first line, the remainder is on the following line and no hyphen is inserted. This is useful for dividing text separated by a slash, such as on/off or and/or.

IMPORT DATA

Inserting a Spreadsheet or a Database File

1. Move the insertion point to the place where you want to insert the imported file.
2. Choose Insert, Spreadsheet/Database, Import.
3. Choose Data Type and select the type of data to be imported from the pop-up list.

4. Choose Import As and select the type—Table, Text, or Merge Data File.
5. Enter the filename in the Filename text box or click on the Filename button.
6. Choose the directory and select the filename.
7. Choose OK enough times to return to the Import Data dialog box.
8. Select Named Ranges or Fields, depending on the data type selected.
9. Choose OK or press ENTER.

Inserts a spreadsheet or database file created in other programs in the current document. You can also use these steps to import ASCII delimited text. When you import ASCII files, you can choose the Field or Record delimiters—Tab, Line Feed, Form Feed, or Carriage Return.

Creating and Editing a Link

1. Move the insertion point to the place where you want to import a file from another program.
2. Choose Insert, Spreadsheet/Database, Create Link.
3. Choose the Data Type to be imported.
4. Choose Table, Text, or Merge Data File in the Link As text box, depending upon the data type of the file to be imported.
5. Enter the filename or click on the Filename button to display a list.
6. Choose a directory and select a filename.
7. Choose OK or press ENTER.
8. Enter appropriate ranges or fields.
9. Choose OK or press ENTER.

Imports data and creates a link. The link allows the imported data in the WordPerfect document to be updated whenever corresponding data is changed in the original file. *See* "Updating a Link." You can change the fields or range by choosing Insert, Spreadsheet/Database, Edit Link and choosing OK.

Note *You can also tailor the link by choosing Options and either Update on Retrieve or Show Link Codes (in the WordPerfect document).*

Updating a Link

1. Choose Insert, Spreadsheet/Database, Update.
2. Choose Yes to Update All Data Links.

Changes the data in the WordPerfect document based on changes made in the original file in another program.

INDENT

Indenting from the Left

1. Move the insertion point to the place where you want to begin paragraph indenting.
2. Choose Layout, Paragraph, Indent. (Or press F7.)
3. Type the text.
4. Press ENTER at the end of the paragraph to end the indent formatting.

Indents all lines of the current paragraph. To indent more than one tab stop, press F7 as many times as you want to indent.

Hanging Indent

1. Move the insertion point to the place where you want to begin a hanging indent.
2. Choose Layout, Paragraph, Hanging Indent. (Or press CTRL+F7.)
3. Type the text.
4. Press ENTER to end the formatting and go to the next line.

Formats the paragraph with the first line even with the left margin and the remaining lines indented one tab stop. You can press CTRL+F7 several times to indent the remaining lines more than one tab stop.

Using a Double Indent

1. Move the insertion point to the place where you want to begin double indenting.
2. Choose Layout, Paragraph, Double Indent. (Or press CTRL+SHIFT+F7.)
3. Type the text.
4. Press ENTER to end the formatting and go to the next line.

Indents all lines of the current paragraph from both left and right margins. You can press CTRL+SHIFT+F7 several times to indent several tab stops from both margins.

INDEX

Marking Text

1. Choose Tools, Index to display the feature bar.
2. Select a word or phrase that you want in the index.
3. Click on the Heading text box to insert the selection as a header (or press ALT+SHIFT+H), or type a different heading for the selection if you like.
4. Click on the Subheading text box (or press ALT+SHIFT+S) to insert the selected text, or type a different subheading for the section.
5. Choose Mark.
6. Repeat these steps for all words or phrases that you want to appear in the index.

Inserts an [Index code] at text that you want in an index.

Note *ALT+SHIFT and the hot key accesses the feature bar option that you want.*

Defining and Generating the Index

1. Move the insertion point to the place where you want to insert the index.
2. Choose Tools, Index to display the feature bar, if it isn't already displayed.
3. Choose Define.
4. Make any changes to the index defaults. (See the following bulleted list.)
5. Choose OK or press ENTER to insert the Index definition code in the document. A message of <<Index will generate here>> appears on the screen.
6. Choose Generate.
7. Choose OK or press ENTER.

Inserts items marked for the index following the definition code [DefMark:Index] in the document. The display depends upon the headings and subheadings that were specified for each entry, and the choices made when you defined the index.

You can make any of the following definition changes:

- *Position* selects, from the pop-up list, the way you want the index entries to be displayed. Choices are to display index entries as text followed by dot leaders and the page number; no numbering (text only); text followed directly by a page number; text followed by a page number in parentheses; or text with page numbers aligned at the right margin.
- *Page Numbering* selects the type of page numbers. Either use the document format for page numbers or choose from the User-Defined Page Number Format. Click on Insert to see the list and choose the type you want. For example, you can insert a chapter number followed by a page number. An example is shown in the box below the Position and Page Numbering buttons. The styles in the example box can be deleted if you decide to change the format before leaving the dialog box.

- *Use* Dash to Show Consecutive Pages places a hyphen between page numbers to display a range.
- *Change* selects styles that can be used for headings or subheadings.
- *Concordance File Filename* selects the concordance file that you want to use to generate the index. *See* "Creating a Concordance File" and "Generating an Index Using a Concordance File."

Creating a Concordance File

1. Open a new blank document.
2. Type each word or phrase that you want in the index on a separate line.
3. Sort the words alphabetically.
4. Save the document.

Saves a list of words that can be used to mark text for an index. This is an efficient way of marking text. When you define the index, WordPerfect will use these words to locate and mark matching words in the document. You only have to type the word or phrase once, and every occurrence of the matching word or phrase in the document will be marked automatically.

Generating an Index Using a Concordance File

1. Move the insertion point to the place where the index is to be inserted.
2. Choose Tools, Index to display the feature bar.
3. Choose Define.
4. Enter the name for the concordance file in the Filename text box, or click on the Filename button and select from the list of filenames, and then choose OK.
5. Choose OK or press ENTER.
6. Choose Generate.
7. Choose OK or press ENTER.

Generates an index at the insertion point using the words in the concordance file to mark the text for the index. Using a concordance file can save a great deal of time, particularly in long documents or where several files, such as chapters in a book, are going to be combined into one document.

INITIAL CODES

Keyboard

1. Choose Layout, Document, Initial Codes Style.

   The Styles Editor dialog box is displayed. InitialStyle is displayed as the Style Name. It is grayed out and can't be changed.
2. Make sure the insertion point is in the Contents box.
3. Use the Styles Editor menu to make changes, and insert the codes in the Contents box.
4. Choose OK or press ENTER when done.

Mouse

1. Triple-click on the initial style code [Open Style: InitialStyle] at the beginning of the document. Then follow the preceding steps 2 through 4.

Sets the formatting, or inserts graphics, tables, other files, or commands that you want to use for the current document. These changes will override the formatting contained in the Standard Template for the current document only. *See also* TEMPLATE and STYLES.

Use the Styles Editor menu the same way you use the WordPerfect menu to insert items, graphics, or tables, or to insert formatting codes. Categories in this menu are Edit, Insert, Layout, Tools, Graphics, and Table.

The code containing the initial code style changes is placed automatically at the top of the document.

INITIAL FONTS

See FONTS

INSERT FILE

1. Move the insertion point to the place where you want to insert a file.
2. Choose Insert, File.
3. Select the name of the file that you want to insert. You can select a file from a different directory if you like: double-click on the directory name and then select the file you want. Also, before selecting a file, you can choose List Files of Type and specify the types of filenames to be displayed.
4. Choose Insert, Yes to insert into current document. If you are inserting a file in a new document window that contains no text, the dialog box asking to choose Yes will not be displayed.

Retrieves a file and places it at the insertion point, which can be at any position in the active document window. This allows you to combine two or more files in one document. It is different from opening a file, which retrieves a file and displays it in a separate document window. *See also* OPEN A DOCUMENT.

ITALIC

Keyboard

1. Move the insertion point to the place where you want to begin formatting in italic.
2. Choose Layout, Font, Italic and press ENTER. (Or Press CTRL+I.)
3. Type the text you want formatted in italic.

Mouse

1. Move the insertion point to the place where you want to begin formatting in italic.
2. Click on the Italic Font button in the Power Bar. A second click will remove italics.
3. Type the text you want formatted in italic.

Formats the text in italic (slanted) characters. To end the formatting, click on the Italic Font button; press CTRL+I; press the RIGHT ARROW key to move the insertion point to the right of the End Italic code; or choose Layout, Font, Italic to turn off the italic formatting. The status bar shows an example of the formatting.

Note *You can also select a block of text and apply italic to it using these same steps.*

JUSTIFICATION

Left Justification

Keyboard

1. Move the insertion point to the place where you want to begin left justification.
2. Choose Layout, Justification, Left. (Or press CTRL+L.)
3. Type the text.

Mouse

1. Move the insertion point to the place where you want to begin left justification.
2. Click on the Justification button in the Power Bar and drag to Left.
3. Type the text.

Aligns all lines of the paragraphs at the left margin. The right margin is ragged. The formatting remains at Left justification until you use these same steps and select a different type of justification.

Left justification is the default formatting for all documents.

Using Right Justification

See FLUSH RIGHT

Using Center Justification

See CENTERING

Using Full Justification

Keyboard

1. Move the insertion point to the place where you want to begin full justification.
2. Choose Layout, Justification, Full. (Or press CTRL+J.)
3. Type the text.

Mouse

1. Move the insertion point to the place where you want to begin full justification.
2. Click on the Justification button in the Power Bar and drag to Full.
3. Type the text.

Begins formatting paragraphs with full justification. Full justification aligns both the left and right ends of the lines at the margins. Extra space is inserted between words to align the text at the margins. This is used frequently in newspaper columns.

Using All Justification

Keyboard

1. Move the insertion point to the place where you want to begin All justification.
2. Choose Layout, Justification, All.
3. Type the text.

Mouse

1. Move the insertion point to the place where you want to begin All justification.
2. Click on the Justification button in the Power Bar and drag to All.
3. Type the text.

Inserts extra space between characters as well as between words so that both the left and right margins are even, regardless of line length. If you press ENTER, the formatting continues to the next paragraph. Use these same steps to change to a different type of justification.

KERNING

1. Move the insertion point *between* the characters where you want to adjust the spacing.
2. Choose Layout, Typesetting, Manual Kerning.
3. Enter a measurement for the Amount or choose from the list.
4. Choose the units of measurement from the Units of Measure pop-up list, if you want to change this.
5. Choose OK or press ENTER.

Manually adjusts the spacing between characters. A horizontal advance code [HAdv] is inserted between the characters, which moves the second character a specific distance to the right. You are limited only by paper size and margins.

Kerning is frequently used in desktop publishing to control the spacing between characters for a "designed" look in headlines or other text elements (*see also* WORD/LETTER SPACING).

KEYBOARD LAYOUT

Selecting a Keyboard Layout

1. Choose File, Preferences, Keyboard.
2. Select the keyboard from the Keyboards list.
3. Choose Select.
4. Choose Close to return to the document window.

Selects a different keyboard layout. A keyboard layout stores the assignments of keys to various features. For example, the default WordPerfect keyboard layout assigns the F3 key to Save As. In a different keyboard layout, the F3 key may be assigned to a different feature.

Creating a Keyboard Layout

1. Choose File, Preferences, Keyboard.
2. Choose Create.
3. Type a name for the new keyboard.
4. Choose Template if you want to assign the keyboard layout to a template where it will be available when that template is used for a document. In the Keyboard Location dialog box, you can assign the new keyboard to either the template that is currently in use, or to the Standard Template, which is the default template used with all documents. Choose OK when done. If you don't want to assign a keyboard layout to a template, skip this step. *See also* TEMPLATE.
5. Choose OK to go to the Keyboard Editor where you can assign keys to WordPerfect features, scripts, and macros. (See the following discussions for making these assignments.)
6. Choose OK to leave the Keyboard Editor.
7. Choose Close and choose Close again to return to the document.

Creates a file where you can store a keyboard layout.

Assigning a WordPerfect Feature from the Keyboard Editor

1. Be sure the Keyboard Editor is displayed. If it is not, choose File, Preferences, Keyboard, select the keyboard to edit, and choose Edit; or choose Create, type a name, and choose OK.
2. Choose Activate a Feature to turn it on. It is probably already selected.
3. Click on the key in the keyboard (displayed at the bottom of the screen) to go quickly to that group, and then select a key from the Choose a Key to Assign or Unassign list.
4. Click on the Feature Categories list.
5. Select a WordPerfect category (menu) item. The options for that menu are then displayed in the Features list box.
6. Select the feature you want to assign to the selected key.
7. Choose Assign Feature. The new assignment is now displayed in the Choose a Key to Assign or Unassign list, and a description is shown at the bottom of the Assign Key to box.
8. Turn on Assignment Appears on Menu if you like.

Designates a key or key combination that is pressed to run a WordPerfect feature. You can also remove a key assignment. To do this, select the key from the Choose a Key to Assign or Unassign, and then choose Unassign.

Assigning a Script from the Keyboard Editor

1. Be sure the Keyboard Editor is displayed. If it is not, choose File, Preferences, Keyboard, select the keyboard to edit, and choose Edit; or choose Create, type a name, and choose OK.
2. Click on the key in the keyboard (displayed at the bottom of the screen) to go quickly to that group, and then select a key from the Choose a Key to Assign or Unassign list.

3. Choose Play a Keyboard Script to turn on and display a text box.
4. Choose "Type the script this key plays" and type the text (script) that will be played when the key is pressed.
5. Choose Assign Script.

Designates a key or key combination that is pressed to insert text at the insertion point.

Assigning a Program from the Keyboard Editor

1. Be sure the Keyboard Editor is displayed. If it is not, choose File, Preferences, Keyboard, select the keyboard to edit, and choose Edit; or choose Create, type a name, and choose OK.
2. Click on the key in the keyboard (displayed at the bottom of the screen) to go quickly to that group, and then select a key from the Choose a Key to Assign or Unassign list.
3. Choose Launch a Program to turn it on.
4. Choose Select File to go to the Select File dialog box.
5. Select the file or program.
6. Choose OK to return to the Keyboard Editor.

Assigns key(s) that can be used to run a program or insert a file at the insertion point in a document. For example, you can use this option to assign a key that creates and displays a frequently-used graphic.

Assigning a Macro from the Keyboard Editor

1. Be sure the Keyboard Editor is displayed. If it is not, choose File, Preferences, Keyboard, select the keyboard to edit, and choose Edit; or choose Create, type a name, and choose OK.
2. Click on the key in the keyboard (displayed at the bottom of the screen) to go quickly to that group, and then select a key from the Choose a Key to Assign or Unassign list.

3. Choose Play a Macro to turn it on.
4. Choose Assign Macro to display the Select Macro dialog box.
5. Enter the macro name to be assigned to the key; or click on the button at the right end of the Name box to go to the Select File dialog box, and select the macro you want. Choose OK to return to the Select Macro dialog box.
6. Choose Select.

Designates a key or key combination that is pressed to play a macro at the insertion point.

Editing a Keyboard Layout

1. Choose File, Preferences, Keyboard.
2. Select the keyboard to be edited. You cannot edit the supplied keyboards.
3. Choose Edit.
4. Make any changes using the procedures just given for assigning keys, or choose Unassign to remove the feature or action from the key.
5. Choose OK to leave the Keyboard Edit dialog box.
6. Choose Close to leave Keyboard Preferences dialog box, then choose Close to leave the Preferences dialog box.

Reassigns keys for the WordPerfect features, scripts, or macros; or removes the feature or action from a key or key combination.

Note *You can also delete a keyboard layout or copy it. In the Keyboard Preferences dialog box, select the keyboard to be deleted or copied. Choose Delete, Yes to remove the keyboard layout name from the list. Choose Copy, select the keyboard to be copied, choose Template to copy to and select the template name, and then choose Copy again.*

LABELS

1. Choose Layout, Labels.
2. Choose the Display—Laser, Tractor-Fed, or Both. Both is the default.
3. Select the label from the Labels list. Most available labels are named here. The details for each are shown below the list box, and an example is shown in the lower-right corner.
4. Choose Select.
5. Type the address in the first label and press ENTER enough times to display the next label.
6. Repeat for as many labels as you need.
7. Choose File, Print, Print or click on the Print button to print. Be sure the printer is online and the labels have been loaded in the printer bin.

Creates a document that is used to address and print labels. Save the document if you use these addresses frequently, or close without saving, after you have printed the labels.

LANDSCAPE ORIENTATION

See PAPER SIZE and PRINTERS

LANGUAGE

1. Move the insertion point to the place where you want to begin using a different language to control certain WordPerfect features.
2. Choose Tools, Language.
3. Select the language from the Current Language list.
4. Choose OK or press ENTER.

Inserts a language code [Lang: xx] at the insertion point. From this position on, features such as sorting, spell checking, date, and time formats will be affected by guidelines based on the selected language. Spelling will be checked on the basis of the language only if you have the correct dictionary for that language.

LETTER SPACING

See WORD/LETTER SPACING

LINE

See GRAPHICS

LINE HEIGHT

1. Move the insertion point to the place where you want to set a line height.
2. Choose Layout, Line, Height.
3. Choose Fixed.
4. Type a measurement or choose from the list.
5. Choose OK or press ENTER.

Inserts a line height code that [Ln Height] sets the line height. When Auto (which is the default) is turned on, the line height is set automatically on the basis of the font that is currently being used. You can change this by entering a specific line height measurement using the steps presented here.

LINE NUMBERING

1. Move the insertion point where you want to begin line numbering.
2. Choose Layout, Line, Numbering.
3. Choose Turn Line Numbering On. Be sure an X is in the box. The default numbering method is shown in the example box.
4. Make any changes. (See choices in the following bulleted list.)
5. Choose OK or press ENTER.

Begins numbering all lines including blank lines. To turn off line numbering, choose Layout, Line, Numbering. If you turn it on again later in the document, numbering will restart at 1.

You can make any of the following changes to the way lines are numbered and to the display:

- *Numbering Method* chooses Numbers, Lowercase letters, Uppercase letters, Lowercase Roman, or Uppercase Roman.
- *Starting Line Number* chooses a starting number. You can also choose numbering intervals here. For example, if you choose 5 as the interval, only lines 1, 6, 11, 16, and so on will be numbered.
- *Position of Numbers*, *From Left Edge of Page*, sets a distance from the left edge of the paper. The default is .6. You can also turn on Left of Margin and specify the distance.
- *Restart Numbering on Each Page* should be turned off to have the numbering be continuous throughout the document. *Restart Numbering on Each Page* is the default.
- *Count Blank Lines* specifies whether or not to count the blank lines between paragraphs.

- *Number All Newspaper Columns* numbers the lines in newspaper columns.
- *Font* specifies a font for the line numbers. The default is to use the same font that is used in the document.

LINE SPACING

Keyboard

1. Move the insertion point to the position where you want to change the line spacing.
2. Choose Layout, Line, Spacing.
3. Enter the Spacing or press the up or down arrow keys to select and change the spacing. An example is shown at the right of the Spacing text box.
4. Choose OK or press ENTER.

Mouse

1. Move the insertion point to the position where you want to change the line spacing.
2. Click on the Line Spacing button in the Power Bar.
3. Select the spacing you want—1.0, 1.5, or 2.0.

Inserts a line spacing code at the left end of the current line and begins new line spacing. Use these same steps to return to your original line spacing, or to select a different line spacing. When you use a mouse and click on the Line Spacing button, you can choose Other to go to the Line Spacing dialog box. Then use the keyboard steps 3 and 4 to specify line spacing other than 1, 1.5, or 2.

LINK

See IMPORT DATA

LISTS

Marking Text

1. Choose Tools, List. The List feature bar is displayed.
2. Type a name for the list in the List text box; for example, Tables, Lists, Figures, Charts, and so on.
3. Select the item in the document that is to be included in the list (a caption, table number, the title of a list, or figure number, for example.)
4. Choose Mark.
5. Repeat steps 3 and 4 for each item to be included in the list. Use the same list name for all selections that are the same type.

Marks items that are to be included in a list similar to an index. An example of this would be if you wanted to produce a list of tables and their page numbers. Select and mark the caption for each table and identify each as "Table" (or use any name you want) in the list box.

You can enter a different name to create a different list. Several lists can be created in one document.

Defining and Generating the List

1. Move the insertion point to the place where you want to display the list.
2. Choose Tools, List if you need to display the feature bar.
3. Choose Define.
4. Choose the List Name.
5. Choose Insert.
6. Choose Generate.
7. Choose OK or press ENTER.

Displays a list of marked items and their page numbers at the place where the definition code is located. If page numbers change in the document, generate the list a second time to display the new page numbers. You do not have to mark the items a second time. The mark codes are still in place.

If you entered more than one list name, use these same steps to generate it at a different position in the document.

Editing the List Characteristics

1. Choose Tools, List to display the feature bar.
2. Choose Define.
3. Select the List Name to be edited.
4. Choose Edit.
5. Change the Numbering Format—select from the pop-up list for changing the Position of the page numbers or the style of Page Numbering.
6. Choose Change, if you like, select the style you want to change, choose Edit, and use the Styles Editor menu to change the style for lists. Choose OK to leave the Styles Editor.
7. Choose Auto Reference Box Captions, if you like, and select a box type from the pop-up list.
8. Choose OK or press ENTER.
9. Choose Close.

Changes the way the output will be displayed when the list is generated. The Retrieve option in the Define List dialog box is used to copy lists that have been in other documents into the current document.

If you choose Auto Reference Box Captions in the Edit List dialog box, choose a box type from the drop-down list that corresponds to graphic boxes in your document. If these boxes have captions, the caption text will be used automatically in a list that is generated without marking the captions. If there are no captions, the boxes will not be included in the list.

LOCATION OF FILES

See DIRECTORIES and PREFERENCES

MACROS

Recording a Macro

1. Choose Tools, Macro, Record. (Or press CTRL+F10.)
2. Type a name for the macro.
3. Choose Record. The status bar now shows Macro Record.
4. Enter the keystrokes, including text, to be stored in the macro. (Mouse actions cannot be used in a macro.)
5. Press CTRL+F10 or choose Tools, Macro, Record to end the macro.

Saves keystrokes that can be played in subsequent documents. Macros are frequently created to save and print documents, create tables, or insert logos or headings in letters. Consider creating a macro for any combination of keys that you use frequently. Macros are similar to abbreviations; however, you can only store text in abbreviations. In macros, besides entering text, you can store keystrokes that perform a variety of WordPerfect functions and commands, and create dialog boxes (*see also* ABBREVIATIONS).

Playing a Macro

1. Move the insertion point to the place where you want to play the macro.
2. Choose Tools, Macro, Play. (Or press ALT+F10.)
3. Enter the macro name or press F4 (or ALT+DOWN ARROW) to go to the Select File dialog box.
4. Select the name of the macro.

5. Choose Play.

Plays, or runs, the keystrokes that have been saved in the macro. In some cases, the placement of the insertion point is not critical to running the macro; for example, if you have a macro that saves and prints, your insertion point can be anyplace when you run the macro.

See KEYBOARD LAYOUT for information about assigning keys to play the macro. It is a good idea to assign keys to frequently used macros. Assigning keys allows you to simply press the keys to play the macro instead of choosing Tools, Macro and then selecting the macro.

Editing a Macro

1. Choose Tools, Macro, Edit.
2. Enter the name of the macro, or press F4 or ALT+DOWN ARROW, select a macro from the Select File dialog box, and choose OK.
3. Choose Edit. The Macro feature bar and the text and commands in the macro are displayed.
4. Make the changes.
5. Choose Close and Yes to save changes.

Displays the contents of the macro, both text and commands. Text can be edited the same way in any document window. The macro feature bar is also displayed and is used to make other changes.

Note *Use the Command Inserter to insert programming commands. The macros are saved in the Standard Template but can be copied or moved to other templates if you like.*

MAIL ENABLE

1. Choose File, Mail. The screen display depends upon the mail system that you are using.
2. Set the mail options that are necessary for your system.
3. Select the document(s) that you want to send. The active document will be automatically attached. Or you

can select a block of text and it will be inserted in the mail system's message box.

4. Send the document(s).
5. Exit to WordPerfect.

Links WordPerfect with your mail system, enabling you to send files or selected text directly from WordPerfect to others on your system.

MARGIN RELEASE (BACK TAB)

1. Move the insertion point to the place where you want to use the margin release.
2. Choose Layout, Paragraph, Back Tab. (Or press SHIFT+TAB.)
3. Type text.
4. Press ENTER to end.

Moves the insertion point one tab stop to the left. At the left margin, you would move one tab stop to the left of the margin, allowing you to enter text in the margin. Using Margin Release places a [Hd Back Tab] code at the insertion point.

MARGINS

Keyboard

1. Move insertion point to the place where you want to change the margins.
2. Choose Layout, Margins. (Or press CTRL+F8.)
3. Enter the measurements for the various margins or press the up or down arrows to select a measurement. An example of the page with the new margins is shown at the right of the Page Margins box.
4. Press ENTER.

Mouse

1. Move the insertion point to the place where you want to change the margins.
2. Choose View, Ruler Bar (or press ALT+SHIFT+F3) to display the ruler if it is not already displayed.
3. Drag the left and right margin markers to different locations; or double-click on either of the margin markers to display the Margin dialog box.
4. Enter measurements for the margins.
5. Choose OK.

Inserts codes for the new left and right margins at the left end of the current line, changing the margins from that point on. Changes to the top and bottom margins will be in effect from the current page on, and the codes for these changes will be inserted automatically at the top of the page.

MARK TEXT

See INDEX, TABLE OF AUTHORITIES, TABLE OF CONTENTS, CROSS-REFERENCE, or LISTS

MASTER DOCUMENTS

Inserting Subdocuments

1. Choose File, Master Document, Subdocument.
2. Select the file to be inserted.
3. Choose Include. A code is inserted in the current document as well as an icon at the left side of the document window.
4. Repeat these steps to insert additional documents.

Inserts subdocument codes [Subdoc] that will retrieve documents and combine them in one master document.

This is useful when generating indexes and tables of contents for a document that contains several chapters. Or if you have an especially large document, it is easier to work with it when it is divided into several smaller documents and then combine them to number the pages consecutively, or to print as one document.

When subdocuments are combined, only codes are inserted in the current document specifying the documents to be combined. You can then expand the documents to see all text, or condense to display only one document at a time. See the following discussions for instructions on how to do this.

Expanding Subdocuments

Keyboard

1. Choose File, Master Document, Expand Master.
2. Press ENTER.

Mouse

1. Double-click on any subdocument icon at the left side of the document window.
2. Choose OK.

Displays text that is in the subdocuments listed in the Expand Master Document dialog box. If you want to expand only one document, choose Mark, Clear All to remove all the Xs in the document check boxes, and then select the one you want to turn on. Be sure an X is displayed in the one(s) you want to expand. The Mark, Mark All option is used to mark all documents again.

Expanding displays the document text, and you can edit the text or make any other changes. A beginning and ending icon are shown at the left side of the window for each expanded document. When you condense, you can also save the edits in the document.

Condensing and Saving Subdocuments

1. Choose File, Master Document, Condense Master.
2. All documents to be condensed and saved are selected (Xs in check boxes). If you want to condense or save only specific documents, select the filename to remove the X for those that you do not want to condense or to save.
3. Choose OK or press ENTER.

Removes document text from the window and saves the document, if you choose to do so. Only the icons are displayed. You may want to go to Reveal Codes to see the code for each document if the icons are overlapping in the window.

If you choose Mark in the Condense/Save Subdocument dialog box, you can then choose to Condense All, Clear Condense, Save All, or Clear Save. The Clear options remove the Xs from the check boxes, and you can then select the specific documents that you want to condense or save.

Saving the Master Document

You can save the master document as a separate file the same way you save other WordPerfect documents. Saving the master document saves the codes that combine the files in the order in which you placed them (*see also* SAVE).

MATH

See TABLES

MENU EDITOR

1. Choose File, Preferences, Menu Bar.
2. Select the menu to edit and choose Edit; or choose Create, type a name for the new menu, and choose OK. You can also choose Template and specify where to save the menu. Choose either Current Template or Default Template.

Displays the Menu Bar Editor dialog box. You can now add items to the menu by dragging them from the dialog box to the menu bar at the top of the screen, or remove items from the menu bar by dragging them away from the menu.

Note *You cannot edit the supplied menus that come with WordPerfect.*

Adding a Feature

1. Turn on Activate a Feature. It may already be on by default.
2. Click on the Feature Categories button and select a menu item. A list of features available for that item will be displayed in the Features box. These include current menu items as well as some that are not in the menu.
3. Click and drag the feature to any position in the menu at the top of the screen. The pointer becomes a hand holding a rectangle. Cascading menus will be displayed as you move the pointer to the menu bar and drag down the list.
4. Release the left mouse button when the item is at the desired position.

Places frequently used features in a specific menu.

Deleting a Feature

1. Point, without holding down the button, to the item in the menu at the top of the screen to select it.

2. Then hold down the left mouse button and drag to any position away from the menu. The pointer becomes a wastebasket with the rectangle dropping into it.
3. Release the left mouse button.

Removes unused features from a menu.

Note *Use these same procedures to insert or delete a separator line in a menu. Drag the Separator icon to the place where you want to insert it, or drag the line away from the menu to remove it.*

Adding a New Item to the Menu Bar

1. Drag the Menu icon to the desired position in the menu at the top of the screen. The word "Menu" is now added to the menu bar.
2. To customize it (or to customize any other item), double-click on the item. The Edit Menu Text dialog box is displayed showing the menu name in the text box.
3. Type a new menu name and type a prompt in the Help Prompt text box, if you like.
4. Choose OK.

Inserts a new item in the menu bar. You can now add features to the menu item. If you typed a prompt, it will show in the status bar when the menu item is selected. You can remove the menu item using the same procedures used to delete a feature.

MERGE

Creating a Data File

Keyboard

1. Choose Tools, Merge. (Or press SHIFT+F9.) (When a block is selected, Merge is not an available menu item.)
2. Choose Data. A Create Data File dialog box appears.
3. Type a field name in the Name a Field text box.

4. Choose Add or press ENTER.
5. Repeat for all additional field names.
6. Choose OK when done to display the Quick Data Entry dialog box.
7. Type appropriate information in the first field.
8. Choose Next Field or press ENTER or TAB.
9. Repeat for each field in the record.
10. Choose New Record or press ENTER to display the next blank record.
11. Repeat steps for entering information in additional records.
12. Choose Close when done.
13. Choose Yes to save, and type a filename for the data file. Choose OK.

Mouse

1. Click on the Merge button in the Button Bar. Then follow the preceding steps 2 through 13.

Creates field names and enters data in each field. These fields will then be placed in the form file at the positions where you want the information to be inserted when the merge is performed.

All information, or fields, pertaining to one individual (company, person, and so on) is a record.

The data file can remain in the document window when you create the form file.

Creating a Form File

Keyboard

1. Choose Tools, Merge; or if the feature bar is displayed, choose Merge to display the Merge dialog box. (Or press SHIFT+F9.)
2. Choose Form.
3. Choose New Document Window.
4. Choose OK or press ENTER.

5. Enter the name of the data file to be associated with it, or click on the button at the end of the Associated Data File text box, select the file from the list, and choose OK.
6. Choose OK or press ENTER to leave the Create Form dialog box.

Mouse

1. Click on the Merge button in the Button Bar. Then follow the preceding steps 2 through 6.

Displays a new blank document window and the Merge feature bar. See the following instructions for inserting fields in the form.

Inserting Fields

1. Move the insertion point to the place where you want to insert a field.
2. Choose Insert Field.
3. Select the field to be inserted.
4. Choose Insert. The Insert Field Name or Number dialog box remains on the screen so that you can insert fields at any time.
5. Move the insertion point to a position for the next field, select the field, and choose Insert. Repeat for any additional fields.
6. Type the boilerplate text that you want in the form.
7. Insert other fields as needed, or insert the same field more than once, if that is appropriate.
8. Choose Close when done to remove the Insert Field Name or Number dialog box.

Creates a form file and displays it in the active window. You can save the form by choosing File, Save As and giving it a name, as you do for other document files.

Merging the Data File and the Form File

1. Be sure the Merge feature bar is displayed.
2. Choose Merge from the feature bar.

3. Choose Merge in the Merge dialog box. The Perform Merge dialog box is displayed.
4. Be sure the documents you want to merge are displayed in the text boxes.
5. Choose OK to merge to a new document window.

Combines information in the data file with the form file and displays it in a document window. You can also choose Output File in the Perform Merge dialog box and type a new filename to save the output to a new file. In addition, you can choose Output File and send the output directly to the printer without taking up disk space, or select an existing file to merge to from a list of files.

Other options in the Perform Merge dialog box that can be chosen when you merge are as follows:

- *Reset* removes all conditions for merging that may be entered in the Select Records dialog box.
- *Select Records* specifies conditions for the merge, such as choosing to merge only records 1 through 5, for example. Or you can choose to merge only those records that contain the same information in certain fields (only those in a specific ZIP code area, for example). Or choose Mark Records and select only those records displayed in the Record List box that you want to include in the merge.
- *Envelopes* enters a return address. The insertion point is in the Mailing Addresses text box. Choose Field, select the field, and choose Insert to insert the appropriate fields in the Mailing Addresses text box. The merge function can then be used to address each envelope based on fields in the data file. You can also insert fields in the Return Addresses text box.
- *Options* separates each document with a page break (the default); specifies the number of copies for each record (if you wanted two copies of each letter, you can set that here); or sets a condition if a field is empty—either leave the field blank, or remove the blank line or space.

Note *If you saved data files and form files previously, you can merge them at a later date by clicking on the Merge button or by choosing Tools, Merge (SHIFT+F9) and then Merge. Enter the filename for the form file, or click on the left arrow, choose Select File, and choose the file from the list of filenames. Enter the filename for the data file or select from the list using this same procedure. Choose the type of output you want and choose OK to merge.*

MOUSE USAGE

See DRAG AND DROP; SELECT TEXT; and GRAPHICS

MOVE

Moving Text

See COPY, CUT, PASTE, and DRAG AND DROP

Moving Files

1. Open a Directory dialog box—choose either File, Open; File, Save As; or Insert, File.
2. Select the file to be moved.
3. Choose File Options.
4. Choose Move.
5. The path and filename of the selected file are displayed in the From text box.
6. Type the path and filename to move to in the To box. If you want to keep the same filename, just type the directory name or the drive name.
7. Choose Move.

Moves the file from the current directory to another location. Use this procedure if you want to move a file from the current WordPerfect directory to a floppy disk, or if you want to move it to another directory on the current disk.

Note *You can move several files at the same time using this same procedure.* See *SELECT for selecting multiple document files. When several files are moved, enter only the path to move files to.*

NEW DOCUMENT

Keyboard

1. Choose File, New. (Or press CTRL+N.)

Mouse

1. Click on the New Document button in the Power Bar.

Displays a new blank document window. The title bar shows a number for the document.

OPEN A DOCUMENT

Keyboard

1. Choose File, Open. (Or press CTRL+O.)
2. Select the filename. (If you move the insertion point into the Filename list, you can then press the first letter of the file to go quickly to it.)
3. Choose OK or press ENTER.

Mouse

1. Click on the Open button in the Power Bar. Then follow the preceding steps 2 through 3.

Displays the contents of the file in the current document window.

OTHER CODES

1. Move the insertion point to the place where you want to insert the codes.
2. Choose Layout, Line, Other Codes.
3. Select the code you want.
4. Choose Insert.

Inserts the selected code at the insertion point. You can choose to insert any of the following types of codes:

- Hard tab codes
- Hard tab codes with dot leaders
- Hyphenation codes (*see also* HYPHENATION)
- Hard space
- End centering/alignment
- Thousands separator

Note *You can insert these codes in macros as well as in text.*

OUTLINE (APPEARANCE)

Keyboard

1. Move the insertion point to the place where you want to begin formatting characters in outline form.
2. Choose Layout, Font. (Or press F9.)
3. Choose Outline. Be sure an X is displayed in the check box.
4. Choose OK or press ENTER.
5. Type the characters.
6. Repeat these same steps to turn off Outline appearance, or press the RIGHT ARROW to move to the right of the end [Outln] code.

Mouse

1. Move the insertion point to the place where you want to begin formatting characters in outline form.
2. Click the right mouse button and choose Font. Then follow the preceding steps 3 through 6.

Formats the characters with an outline appearance if your printer is capable of printing characters with this format. The text may or may not be displayed on the screen as outline characters, and this also depends upon the printer that is selected.

Note *You can also select text and use these steps to apply the formatting to the selection.*

OUTLINING

Displaying the Feature Bar to Create an Outline

1. Move the insertion point to the place where you want to begin outlining.
2. Choose Tools, Outline.

Displays the Outline feature bar and inserts the first outline level in the document. Outline levels and text are identified at the left side of the window.

Entering Text for the Outline Levels

Keyboard

1. Type the text for the first level and press ENTER. The same level is repeated.
2. Press TAB to move to the next level.
3. Type the text for it and press ENTER.
4. Press SHIFT+TAB to move back a level and enter text, pressing ENTER at the end of the text.
5. Press CTRL+H or ALT+SHIFT+T if you want to change to text.

6. Press CTRL+H or ALT+SHIFT+T to return to an outline level.

Mouse

1. Type the text for the level and press ENTER.
2. Click on the Right Arrow button in the feature bar to go to the next level.
3. Type text and press ENTER.
4. Click on the Left Arrow button in the feature bar to go back to the previous level.
5. Click on the Up Arrow button to move the paragraph up and keep the same level.
6. Click on the Down Arrow button to move the paragraph down and keep the same level.
7. Click on the *T* button to change the level to body text. Click on the *T* button again to return body text to the outline level.

Inserts outline levels and formats text as an outline. To turn off outlining, choose Options, End Outline. If the Outline feature bar remains displayed in the window, you can begin outlining again in the same document by choosing Options, Change Level, selecting the level number from the list, and choosing OK.

Selecting the Outline Levels to be Displayed

Keyboard

1. Be sure the Outline feature bar is displayed in the window.
2. Press ALT+SHIFT plus the underlined characters to access buttons in the feature bar and select the outline level.

Mouse

1. Be sure the Outline feature bar is displayed in the window.

2. Click on any of the number buttons to show the outline levels from 1 through the selected number.
3. Click on the All button to show all levels.
4. Select the outline levels and click on the plus (+) button to show all outline family members, which consists of all level numbers plus text.
5. Select the outline levels and click on the minus (-) button to show only outline levels. Text levels are not displayed.

Changes the display in the window. This is helpful when you are working in a specific section of a document, and do not need to see other sections.

Selecting an Outline Style

Keyboard

1. Display the Outline feature bar and move the insertion point to the level where you want to change the outline style, or select all levels you want to change. Paragraph is the default style.
2. Choose Options (Press ALT+SHIFT+O).
3. Choose Define Outline.
4. Select the style from the Name list box. If you have not selected a block of outline levels in the document, but want to begin using a different style, choose Start New Outline to turn it on.
5. Choose OK or press ENTER.

Mouse

1. Display the Outline feature bar and move the insertion point to the level where you want to change the outline style, or select a block of outline levels you want to change. Paragraph is the default style.
2. Click on the arrow at the right of the Outline Styles text box. (It probably shows Paragraph as the style name.)
3. Choose the outline style you want.

Applies a new style to the outline from the insertion point forward or applies it to selected levels. The choices of outline styles are the following.

- *Bullets* uses various styles of bullets to mark outline levels.
- *Headings* centers the main headings and formats all headings in bold.
- *Legal* numbers outline levels with 1, 1-1, and so on.
- *Legal 2* numbers outline levels with 1, 1.01, and so on.
- *Numbers* uses numbers and lowercase letters for outline levels.
- *Outline* uses Roman numerals, letters, and numbers for outline levels.
- *Paragraph* is the default and uses numbers and lowercase letters to designate outline levels.

Defining an Outline Style

1. Be sure the Outline feature bar is displayed.
2. Choose Options.
3. Choose Define Outline.
4. Select an outline style and choose Edit, or choose Create. Type a new name and description for the style.
5. Make changes in the Edit Outline Definition dialog box. (See the list of options in the following bulleted list.)
6. Choose OK to save changes and leave the Edit Outline Definition dialog box.
7. Choose OK or press ENTER to leave the Outline Define dialog box. If a new style was created, it is added to the Outline Styles list in the feature bar. (Choose Close to leave without saving the changes.)
8. Choose Close to remove the feature bar.

Changes the format of an existing outline style, or creates a new style that is saved and can be used in other documents.

You can choose any of the following outline style options in the Edit Outline Definition dialog box:

- *Levels* selects the outline level you want to include in the style.

- *Associated Style* selects the style associated with the selected level. The choice is automatic when you select a level, however, you can change that by selecting a different associated style.
- *Custom Number* selects the style for displaying outline numbers or characters. Press on the arrow at the right of the text box to choose the style. Repeat for each level and make individual changes, if you like.
- *Quick Numbers* chooses a type for the entire outline. The list box below Levels displays the results.
- *Options* changes the list of Associated Styles. You can choose to display Numbers and Styles, Numbers Only, or Styles Only.
- *Create Style* goes to the Styles Editor where you can create a new style.
- *Edit Style* goes to the Styles Editor where you can edit or change the selected style level and the characteristics applied to it.

Note *You can reset any change to the default outline settings by choosing Options from the feature bar, and choose Define Outline to display the Outline Define dialog box. Then select the style displayed in the Name box that was changed, and choose Options, Reset, Yes to restore.*

OVERSTRIKE

1. Move the insertion point to the place where you want to place overstrike characters.
2. Choose Layout, Typesetting, Overstrike.
3. Type the characters for the overstrike character.
4. If you want to format overstrike characters differently from other text, click on the arrow at the right of the Characters text box and choose the format that you want for them. Be sure the characters are then entered between the on and off codes. You also can press

CTRL+W and choose a character set for the overstrike characters. (*See also* CHARACTERS.)

5. Type the text between the On and Off codes in the Characters text box. You can also delete codes and text in the Characters text box.
6. Choose OK or press ENTER when done.

Inserts the overstrike characters at the insertion point. They are displayed the way they will be printed.

Use Overstrike to combine and produce characters that are not available on the keyboard or that are not WordPerfect characters. For example, if you want to insert a zero (0) with a slash through it, type the zero (**0**) followed by a slash (**/**). When you return to the document window, the overstrike character will be displayed.

Note *To edit the characters, double-click on the overstrike code in Reveal Codes (ALT+F3) to display the overstrike dialog box. Make desired changes and choose OK.*

PAGE BORDERS

See BORDERS

PAGE BREAK

1. Move the insertion point to the place where you want to insert the page break.
2. Choose Insert, Page Break. (Or press CTRL+ENTER.)

Ends a page and inserts a double line in the document window indicating the beginning of the next page. A Hard Page code [HPg] is displayed in Reveal Codes at the bottom of the page. Insert a hard page break when you want to manually control the length of the current page.

Normally, pages are ended automatically with a soft page break when enough lines of text, graphics, or tables have been entered to fill one page.

Note *You can also insert a page break in a column to manually end a column and move text to the next column (or the next page if you are in the last column on the page).*

PAGE NUMBERING

Inserting Page Numbering

1. Move the insertion point to any place on the page where you want to begin numbering. If the cursor is on page 3 and you invoke page numbering, then pages 1 and 2 will have no numbers.
2. Choose Layout, Page, Numbering.
3. Choose Position and select the page number position from the list. An example is displayed in the boxes.
4. Choose OK.

Inserts a page number at the selected position. Page numbering continues until you use these same steps and choose No Page Numbering for the Position. You can also stop page numbering on a specific page by choosing Layout, Page, Suppress. When you go to the next page, the page numbers will be displayed again (*see* SUPPRESS).

Changing the Page Numbers

1. Move the insertion point to the page where you want to change the page numbers.
2. Choose Layout, Page, Numbering.
3. Choose a Position.
4. Choose Value.
5. Choose New Page Number and select a new number from the list.
6. Choose OK.

7. Choose Close.

Begins page numbering with the new number on the page where the insertion point is located. Subsequent pages will be renumbered on the basis of the new number.

If you are using additional types of numbering—Chapter, Secondary, or Volume—you can change the values for those settings the same way you change the values for page numbering. Each setting contains an option, Insert and Display at Insertion Point. When this is turned on, a number will be inserted at the insertion point, regardless of where it is positioned on the page, as well as being inserted at the specified position for page number.

Changing the Type of Numbering

1. Move the insertion point to the page where you want to change the type of page numbering.
2. Choose Layout, Page, Numbering.
3. Select a Position if one is not already selected.
4. Choose Options.
5. Click on Page, Secondary, Chapter, or Volume (see list below for descriptions); and select a style of numbering or letters for that type.
6. Choose Insert and select the corresponding number type. It is displayed in the text box and sample pages are shown at the bottom of the dialog box.
7. Choose another number type, if you like, using this same procedure.
8. Choose OK enough times to return to the document window.

Inserts various types of page numbering at the position that is selected in the Page Numbering dialog box. The types available are

- *Page* inserts numbers in consecutive order.
- *Secondary* also inserts numbers similar to page numbers in consecutive order. Use Secondary when you want to display two sets of numbers; for example, Page (#), Next

Page (#). Choose Page as the type for the first number and Secondary as the type for the second number. In the Value dialog box, set the value for the Secondary number to correspond to that of the next page—where the Page # value is 1, the Secondary # value would be set at 2.

- *Volume* inserts numbers that are not incremented automatically. In the Value dialog box, set the number manually. Volumes often refer to sets of periodicals or to groups of chapters or books.
- *Chapter* inserts numbers that are similar to Volume numbers. They do not increment automatically. Set the number manually in the Value dialog box. If you are writing a book that has several chapters, it is usually a good idea to create a separate document for each chapter. The chapter number would remain the same throughout one document.

The styles available for each type of numbering are Numbers, Lowercase Letters, Uppercase Letters, Lowercase Roman, and Uppercase Roman.

You also can include text with page numbering while you are in the Page Numbering Options dialog box. Choose Format and Accompanying Text, type the text that is to appear with the number, and insert the type of number. For example, type **Page** and a space. Then insert a page type number code [Pg #]. An example is displayed in the boxes. All formatting and text can be removed from the text box by selecting it and pressing DEL.

PAGE VIEW

1. Choose View, Page. (Or press ALT+F5.)

Displays the document page as it will be printed. All text and features such as headers and footers, watermarks, and footnotes—everything that will be printed—is shown in the document window.

Working in Page view is slower than working in Draft view because more information is showing.

Viewing Two Pages

1. Choose View, Two Page.

Displays two entire pages in the window. You can enter and edit text and use any WordPerfect features; however, it is difficult to see specific character formatting. This can be helpful in confirming placement of headers and footers, page numbers, footnotes, and end notes. Press ALT+F5 to return to Page view, or press CTRL+F5 to choose Draft view (*see also* ZOOM).

PAPER SIZE

Selecting a Paper Definition

1. Move the insertion point to the page where you want to change the paper size.
2. Choose Layout, Page, Paper Size.
3. Select a paper definition from the Paper Definitions list. An example is shown in the Orientation box, and details, such as size, type, and location are shown in the Information box.
4. Choose Select.

Changes the paper size for the current and the subsequent pages. If you click on the Page Zoom Full button in the Power Bar, you will see the whole page in the window. Click on the button again to return to page view. The paper size code [Paper Sz/Typ] is placed automatically at the top of the current page.

Use these steps to choose a landscape definition, which means that the page will be wider than it is long. (The default page is portrait orientation in which the paper is longer that it is wide.) The way landscape documents are printed depends on the printer. With some printers, you may have to reinsert your paper. In most laser printers, however, the paper is inserted the same way it is for portrait orientation, and characters are rotated 90 degrees when printed. A variety of landscape paper definitions are listed in the Paper Size dialog box.

Creating and Editing a Paper Definition

1. Choose Layout, Page, Paper Size.
2. Choose Create.
3. Type a name for the definition in the Paper Name text box.
4. Make changes appropriate to the definition that fits the paper you will be using (see the following list of options).
5. Choose OK to save the changes and return to the Paper Size dialog box. The new definition name is added to the list of paper definitions.
6. Choose Close to return to the document.

Creates a paper definition tailored to your specific needs. The new definition name is added to the list in the Paper Size dialog box. Later, when you want to use the type of paper defined, go to the Paper Size dialog box and select it.

Options that can be included in the definition are

- *Paper Type* shows a list of various types of paper from which you can choose the one you want.
- *Paper Size* shows a list of paper sizes from which you can choose the one you want, or you can enter specific measurements in the size boxes.
- *Paper Location* shows a list of available choices depending on the type of printer you are using.
- *Rotated Font* can be turned on to rotate the print 90 degrees.
- *Wide Form* changes the definition to landscape—the paper is wider than it is long.
- *Top and Side* adjust text up or down, or to the left or right side. You can enter specific measurements for

these adjustments. Use this when the selected printer does not print the text at specified margins because of hardware incompatibility.

A paper definition can be edited using these same steps—after selecting the paper definition to be changed, choose Edit, or choose Delete to remove the definition.

PARAGRAPH SPACING

1. Move the insertion point to the paragraph where you want to change the spacing following it, or select the paragraph(s) you wish to change.
2. Choose Layout, Paragraph, Format.
3. Choose Spacing Between Paragraphs.
4. Click on the arrows to change values.
5. Choose OK.

Inserts a specified number of lines between paragraphs. To end this formatting, choose Layout, Paragraph, Format and choose Clear All; or set a different number for the paragraph spacing.

PASSWORD

Adding a Password

1. Choose File, Save As. (Or press F3.)
2. Select the filename, or type a new filename if you are saving the current document.
3. Choose Password Protect. Be sure an X is displayed in the box.
4. Choose OK. If you are adding a password to an existing file, a prompt will ask if you want to replace it. Choose Yes.

5. Type the password. You will not see the text. Asterisks are shown to represent the characters. You can enter up to 25 characters, and spaces are allowed.
6. Choose OK.
7. Type the password again to confirm.
8. Choose OK.

Assigns a password to the document, which, from this point on, can only be opened by entering the password and the document is saved as a read-only file. It is important that you remember your password because there is no place in WordPerfect where you can locate it.

Using a Password to Open the Document

Keyboard

1. Choose File, Open. (Or press CTRL+O.)
2. Select the file to be opened. A description [Password Locked] is displayed in the lower left corner of the Open file dialog box.
3. Choose OK or press ENTER.
4. Type the password in the text box.
5. Choose OK or press ENTER.
6. Choose Yes to open as a read-only file.

Mouse

1. Click on the Open button in the Power Bar to go to the Open File dialog box. Then follow the preceding steps 2 through 6.

Retrieves a document file that is password protected. You can edit the document, but it must be saved with a new name to save the change.

Removing a Password

1. Choose File, Save As. (Or press F3.)
2. Select the filename containing the password.

3. Choose Password Protect to turn it off. (The X is removed from the check box.)
4. Choose OK and Yes to replace the file. (It will be saved without the password.)

Removes the assigned password, providing unlimited access to the file.

PASTE

Keyboard

1. Move the insertion point to the place where you want to insert Clipboard contents.
2. Choose Edit, Paste. (Or press CTRL+V.)

Mouse

1. Move the insertion point to the place where you want to insert Clipboard contents.
2. Click on the Paste button in the Power Bar.

Inserts the contents of the Clipboard at the insertion point. If the Clipboard is empty, nothing is pasted. In fact, in the Edit menu, Paste will be in a lighter shade than other options that can be chosen; and in the Power Bar, the Paste button will be dim, also indicating the Clipboard is empty.

Selected text is placed in the Clipboard by choosing Edit and Cut, Copy, or Append (*see also* CUT, COPY, and APPEND).

Note *To insert the Clipboard contents in a data type that you choose from the list in the Paste Special dialog box, choose Edit, Paste Special.*

PREFERENCES

1. Choose File, Preferences.

2. Choose the type of preference. (Double-click on it, or select it and press ENTER.)
3. Make changes in the corresponding dialog box.
4. Choose OK when done to return to the Preferences dialog box.
5. Choose Close to return to the document.

Changes default settings in the various preferences dialog boxes. These changes are permanent (at least until you use Preferences to make further changes); whereas preference changes that are made in the document window are only saved with the current document. When you open another window or when you start WordPerfect the next time, they will return to the original default settings unless you make changes using File, Preferences.

The following are items that can be changed in File, Preferences:

- *Display* designates the features such as Reveal Codes, View/Zoom, Comments, or graphics that are always shown on the screen.
- *Environment* affects some features as you work in the document window. You can set beep options, control the features that are displayed in menus, control hyphenation prompts, and enter a name that can be used when documents are saved. The Code Page option is used to select the character set that is used in documents. Character sets are different for different languages.
- *File* sets backup files and timed backups, and specifies locations of various types of files. This can be changed by selecting the type of file—the path will be displayed in the Default Directory text box— and entering a new path for the file type.
- *Summary* sets search options for documents based on information in the summary.
- *Button Bar* selects the Button Bar to be displayed, as well as modifying each button bar, and customizing both buttons and the bars themselves.

- *Power Bar* changes the items included in the Power Bar. Instructions for making changes are shown at the top of the Power Bar Preferences dialog box.
- *Status Bar* changes the items shown in the status bar. Instructions for making changes are shown at the top of the Status Bar Preferences dialog box. Items that you add are displayed at the right end of the status bar. Drag the item to a different position in the status bar before selecting additional items.
- *Keyboard* changes the keyboard layout (*see* KEYBOARD LAYOUT).
- *Menu Bar* changes the display of items in menus (*see* MENU EDITOR).
- *Writing Tools* selects the tools that are displayed in the Tools menu. Choose Setup and make the changes you want.
- *Print* sets defaults for print specifications such as number of copies, size ratio for fonts when Fine, Small, Large, and so on, are selected. It also sets print quality and color.
- *Import* sets default delimiters and Windows Metafile Options.

PRINT

See also PRINTERS

Keyboard

1. Choose File, Print. (Or press F5.)
2. If you like, make any changes in the Print dialog box (see the following list of options).
3. Choose Print.

Mouse

1. Click on the Print button in the Power Bar. Then follow the preceding steps 2 and 3.

Prints the full document that is in the active window. You can also press CTRL+P to print the current document without going to the Print dialog box.

You can make the following changes in the Print dialog box before printing the current document:

- *Current Page* prints the page where the insertion point is located.
- *Multiple Pages* prints a range of pages. Choose Print after choosing Multiple Pages and type the range. For example, **1-5** prints pages 1 through 5; **1,3,5** prints pages 1, 3, and 5; **1-3,5,7** prints pages 1 through 3 and also pages 5 and 7.
- *Selected Text* prints a block of text that is currently selected.
- *Document Summary* prints the document summary only.
- *Document on Disk* prints a document that is not in the active window, but is saved on a disk. The filename is entered to specify the document to be printed.
- *Number of Copies* sets the number of copies of the document; or if you are printing a range of pages, this can be used to specify the number of pages to print.
- *Generated by* determines the order in which pages are printed. The default is WordPerfect, which means that pages will be collated; for example, if the number of copies is set at 2, the pages will be printed 1, 2, and 3, then 1, 2, and 3. If Printer is chosen, the pages will be printed 1,1; 2,2; 3,3.
- *Print Quality* in *Document Settings* specifies how your document will look when printed. The choices here are High, Medium, or Draft.
- *Print Color* in *Document Settings* specifies colors for printing if your printer is capable of printing in color.
- *Do Not Print Graphics* turns off graphics printing. You may want to do this to save time in printing early drafts of a document.

PRINTERS

Selecting a Printer

1. Choose File, Select Printer.
2. Select the printer you want.
3. Choose Select.

Selects a printer to be used. This is the selected printer until you choose another, even if you exit from WordPerfect.

You can choose Add Printer to install additional printer files, or choose Delete to remove selected printer files.

Changing Initial Fonts

1. Choose File, Select Printer.
2. Choose Initial Font.
3. Select a font for printing.
4. Choose OK or press ENTER.

Selects a different font for all documents; however, if the document initial font is different, it overrides the printer initial font. Also the initial font in the template overrides the printer initial font.

Changing the Printer Setup

1. Choose File, Select Printer.
2. Choose Setup.
3. Make changes.
4. Choose OK.

Makes permanent changes to the specifications for the printer. The options available in the dialog box depend upon the type of printer that is selected.

To print documents with landscape orientation, choose Landscape in the Setup dialog box for the selected printer.

QUICKFINDER

Creating a File Index

1. Choose File, QuickFinder.
2. Choose Indexer.
3. Choose Create.
4. Type a name for the index.
5. Choose OK.
6. Enter the name of the directory in the Add Directory or File text box, or choose Browse and select the directory from the list.
7. Choose Add. Additional directories can now be added using steps 1 through 7.
8. Choose Generate.
9. Choose OK when the indexing is complete. A dialog box will show the progress of the indexing.
10. Choose Close, or choose Create again and use these same steps to create another index.

Creates an index that can be selected at any time to locate files quickly on the basis of text contained in those files. For example, if you have a number of files in a directory that relate to each other—perhaps they are named "Chap1," "Chap2," "Chap3," and so on—in step 6, you would enter the path and filename, **c:\wpwin6.0\data\chap*.***. Only the files beginning with "Chap" will be included in the index, and you can then use QuickFinder to find text in that group of files.

You can follow this same procedure using the WordPerfect QuickFinder icon in the Windows Program Manager to index files outside of WordPerfect.

Using a QuickFinder Index

1. Choose File, QuickFinder.
2. Choose Search In and select QuickFinder Index from the pop-up list.

3. Click on the arrow at the right end of the Search In text box and select the index name. The indexes you created are listed here.
4. Choose Search For and type a word or phrase you want to find.
5. Choose Find. The list of files that contain that word or phrase is displayed.
6. Select a file.
7. Choose View to see the contents of the file. Every occurrence of the word entered in the Search For box is highlighted. You can work with the View window the same way you work with other WordPerfect windows to maximize, move, size, and restore it to its original size, or to close it.
8. Choose Close to leave QuickFinder.

Locates files containing specific words or phrases. When the filenames are displayed in QuickFinder, you can open the files as well as view them.

QUICKFORMAT

This feature requires a mouse.

Mouse

1. Select a block of text containing the formatting characteristics you want to copy.
2. Click on the QuickFormat button in the Button Bar, or choose Layout, QuickFormat. The pointer now shows a paint roller.
3. Drag the paint roller over the text that you want to apply the formatting to and release the left mouse button when done.
4. Repeat step 3 to apply the same formatting to other text.
5. Click on the QuickFormat button, or choose Layout, QuickFormat to turn it off and restore the normal pointer.

Copies formatting from one area of text and applies it quickly to another selection. This is a quick way of adding bold or whatever attributes you want without going to the menu. It also assures consistency in formatting.

If you click on the QuickFormat button, or choose Layout, QuickFormat before selecting a block of text, you can choose whether to apply only Fonts & Attributes, Paragraph Styles, or Both. Both is the default. If you are *not* using paragraph styles, the Paragraph Styles choice will have no effect in QuickFormat.

QUICKLIST

Creating a QuickList

1. Choose either File, Save As; File, Open; or Insert, File to display a Directory dialog box.
2. Choose QuickList and choose Show QuickList if it is not displayed.
3. Choose QuickList, Add Item.
4. Enter the directory name and filenames to be included in the QuickList. For example, enter **c:\wpwin60\wpdocs\doc*.*** to select those files in the WPDOCS directory beginning with "doc" as the filename. Or you can click on the button at the right end of the Directory/Filename text box and select the directory you want. Then specify the files to be included in the QuickList.
5. Click on the Description text box to repeat the directory and filename entered in step 4.
6. Choose OK enough times to return to the document.

Creates a list that can be used in other word processing sessions when searching for specific files. You may want to create a QuickList of memos, or letters, or letters to specific departments or companies. Keep this in mind when you are naming files so that it will be easy to create a QuickList for them.

Using the QuickList

1. Choose either File, Save As; File, Open; or Insert, File to display a Directory dialog box.
2. Choose QuickList.
3. Choose either Show QuickList or Show Both. Show Both will display the QuickList and the directory list. Show Directories is the default.
4. Choose OK.
5. Double-click on the directory/filename in the QuickList box to display the filenames.

Displays documents included in the selected QuickList. The display in the Directory dialog box remains the same until QuickList is chosen and the display is changed.

QUICKMARK

Inserting a QuickMark

1. Move the insertion point to the place where you want to insert the mark.
2. Choose Insert, Bookmark, Set QuickMark. (Or press CTRL+SHIFT+Q.)

Places a QuickMark code at the insertion point. Text is not selected for this, and only one QuickMark can be inserted in the active document. When a second QuickMark is inserted, the previous one is deleted. The difference between a bookmark and a QuickMark is that a file can have multiple bookmarks, but only one QuickMark at a time.

Using a QuickMark

1. Choose Insert, Bookmark, Find QuickMark. (Or press CTRL+Q.)

Moves the insertion point directly to the QuickMark.

Note *You can also choose Edit, Go To, Bookmark, select QuickMark and choose OK.*

QUICKMENU

This feature requires a mouse.

Mouse

1. Press the right mouse button to display a list of options.
2. Choose the option you want and release the mouse button.

Displays a list of options that are used frequently in WordPerfect documents.

The options that are displayed vary depending upon the pointer position when the right mouse button is pressed.

REDISPLAY

See EQUATION

REDLINE

Keyboard

1. Move the insertion point to the place where you want to begin redlining.
2. Choose Layout, Font. (Or press F9.)
3. Choose Redline.
4. Choose OK.
5. Type the text formatted with redlining.

6. Choose Layout, Font, Redline to end the formatting or press the RIGHT ARROW key to move the insertion point to the right of the end code. You may have to go to Reveal Codes to do this.

Mouse

1. Move the insertion point to the place where you want to begin redlining.
2. Click the right mouse button and choose Font. Then follow the preceding steps 3 through 6.

Applies redlining to text. This is used frequently to mark text in a rough draft that has been added to existing text, or that is going to be deleted. Its purpose is to call attention to specific areas of text. Depending upon the printer, the redlined text may be shaded when printed. Use these same steps to apply redlining to a selected block of text.

REPEAT

1. Move the insertion point to the place where you want to repeat a keystroke. This can be any character key, arrow key, ENTER, TAB, BACKSPACE, or DELETE.
2. Choose Edit, Repeat. (Or press SHIFT+F10.)
3. Enter the number of times you want to repeat the keystroke, or choose from the list. (Eight is the default.)
4. Choose OK.
5. Press the key that you want to be repeated.

Repeats any key action. For example, you can use this feature to move the insertion point a specific number of spaces to the left or right, or up or down a specific number of lines. To do this press one of the arrow keys, and it will move automatically the number of times that was entered in the Edit Repeat dialog box. You can also use this procedure if you want to enter a line of asterisks, equal signs, or hyphens, or if you want to use Enter, Backspace, Tab, or Delete a specific number of times.

REPLACE

1. Move the insertion point to the place where you want to begin replacing text.
2. Choose Edit, Replace. (Or press CTRL+F2.)
3. Enter the text to be replaced in the Find text box.
4. Choose Replace With and enter the text to replace with.
5. Choose Replace to locate the first occurrence of the word. It will be highlighted.
6. Choose Replace to replace the word and go to the next occurrence of the word.
7. Repeat these steps to the end of the text, or choose Replace All to replace all occurrences of the word in the document.

Replaces the word or phrase with different text. The Replace feature can also be used with selected text. You can choose to replace fonts or other formatting codes, as well as text.

The following options in the menu bar can be chosen to tailor the Replace feature.

- *Type* selects whether to replace Text or Specific Codes. A list of codes is displayed. Specific Codes contain a value such as a font size, for example.
- *Match* designates the conditions of the search before you enter the Find information. It can be for Whole Word, Case, Font, (a dialog box is displayed) or Codes (a list of codes is displayed).
- *Replace* designates the conditions of the search. It can be for Case, Font, or Codes. This is similar to Match, but it is used after you enter information in the Find and Replace With text boxes.

- *Direction* sets the direction of the search either Forward or Backward.
- *Options* specifies where the search will look, as well as the number of changes allowed.

RETURNS

Inserting Hard Returns

1. Move the insertion point to the place where you want to end the line.
2. Press ENTER to insert a hard return.

Inserts a hard return code [HRt] at the insertion point. This manually ends the current line before text reaches the right margin.

Inserting Soft Returns

1. Type text without pressing ENTER at the ends of lines.

Wraps text automatically to the next line when the right margin is reached. A soft return code [SRt] is inserted at the place where text is moved to the following line.

REVEAL CODES

Keyboard

1. Choose View, Reveal Codes. (Or press ALT+F3.)

Mouse

1. Point to the black bar at the top or bottom of the vertical scroll bar. The pointer becomes a two-sided arrow.
2. Hold down the left mouse button and drag the double line to a position you want, and release the button.

Displays text plus codes. Often, as you are editing, you need to see where you started certain formatting, and you can only see these codes when Reveal Codes is turned on. You can edit text as well as codes in Reveal Codes, if you like. To delete a code, drag it out of the Reveal Codes window or select the code and press DELETE.

To restore the full document window, repeat the steps above; or click with the *right* mouse button in the Reveal Codes window and choose Hide Reveal Codes.

RULER BAR

1. Choose View, Ruler Bar. (Or press ALT+SHIFT+F3.)

Displays the ruler bar in the active window. The ruler bar shows current margins and tab settings while you are entering and editing text.

Use it to change the left or right margins—just drag the margin markers to new positions. (*See also* MARGINS.)

Also use the ruler bar to change tab settings—drag the tabs to different positions, or click on the ruler at the position where you want to insert new tabs. (*See* TABS for complete instructions on doing this.)

SAVE

Keyboard

1. Choose File, Save As. (Or press F3.)
2. Type a filename in the text box.
3. Choose OK.

Mouse

1. Click on the Save button in the Power Bar. Then follow the preceding steps 2 and 3.

Names and saves the document in the active window. If the document has been named previously, and current edits need to be saved, choose File, Save; press CTRL+S;

or click on the Save button. The edits will be automatically saved.

SEARCH

See FIND

SELECT TEXT

Using the Edit, Select Menu

1. Move the insertion point to any sentence, paragraph, or anyplace in the document.
2. Choose Edit, Select.
3. Choose Sentence, Paragraph, Page, or All depending upon what you want to select.

Highlights specified blocks of text (*see also* "Selecting a Tabular Column" later in this section).

Using the Keyboard to Select Text

Use any of the following procedures:

Selection	Keypress
Character to the right	SHIFT+RIGHT ARROW
Character to the left	SHIFT+LEFT ARROW
Word right	SHIFT+CTRL+RIGHT ARROW
Word left	SHIFT+CTRL+LEFT ARROW
One line up	SHIFT+UP ARROW
One line down	SHIFT+DOWN ARROW
Paragraph up from the insertion point	SHIFT+CTRL+UP ARROW
Paragraph down from the insertion point	SHIFT+CTRL+DOWN ARROW

From the insertion point to:

Selection	Keypress
End of line	SHIFT+END
Beginning of line	SHIFT+HOME
End of document	SHIFT+CTRL+END
Beginning of document	SHIFT+CTRL+HOME
First line of previous page	SHIFT+ALT+PAGE UP
First line of next page	SHIFT+ALT+PAGE DOWN

Highlights text, which can then be cut or copied; formatted with different fonts, appearance attributes, paragraph formatting; or used with a variety of other WordPerfect features.

Note *You can also press F8 to toggle Select mode on or off. The word "Select" is a bold shade in the status bar when Select mode is on. In Select mode, move the insertion point to the end of the text to be selected, or use any of the keystrokes listed above without pressing the SHIFT key.*

Using the Mouse to Select Text

Point to the position to begin the selection and drag to the last character, or use any of the following:

Selection	Mouse Action
Word	Double-click on the word
Sentence	Triple-click on the sentence
Paragraph	Click four times on the paragraph or double-click in the left margin.
From the insertion point to the pointer	SHIFT+click
Graphic	Click on it

Highlights selected text. A selected graphic is shown with an outline around it, and handles are displayed on each corner and on each side.

Selecting a Tabular Column

1. Select the column from the first character at the top left to the last character at the bottom right of the column. (All columns will be highlighted.)
2. Choose Edit, Select.
3. Choose Tabular Column.

Selects columns separated by tabs. The column can then be moved using Cut (CTRL+X), Copy (CTRL+C), Paste (CTRL+V), or using the mouse to drag and drop.

Choose Rectangle to move columns that are separated by spaces rather than tabs.

Using the Mouse to Select Several Files in a Directory Dialog Box

Selection	Mouse Action
Select continuous files	Point to the first filename and drag to the last one you want. Or click on the first filename, hold down the SHIFT key, and click on the last filename.
Select noncontinuous files	Hold down the CTRL key and click on each filename

Selects several filenames at once.

Note *A directory dialog box can be used to copy, move, rename, print, or delete one or several files. It can be accessed by choosing File, Save As; File, Open; or Insert, File, and then choosing File Options.*

SHADOW

Keyboard

1. Move the insertion point where you want to begin formatting text.
2. Choose Layout, Font. (Or press F9.)
3. Choose Shadow.
4. Choose OK.
5. Type the text to be formatted with a shadow appearance.
6. Choose Layout, Font, Shadow to end formatting, or press the RIGHT ARROW to move the insertion point to the right of the end code. You may have to turn on Reveal Codes for this.

Mouse

1. Move the insertion point where you want to begin formatting text.
2. Click the right mouse button and choose Font. Then follow the preceding steps 3 through 6.

Formats text with a shadow appearance. This is used frequently in headings or special text that you want to emphasize. You can also select a block of text and use these same steps to apply formatting to the selection.

SHOW

1. Choose View, Show ¶. (Or press CTRL+SHIFT+F3.)

Toggles Show on and off in the active window—other windows are not affected. When Show is on, paragraph marks that are inserted when ENTER is pressed are displayed, as well as symbols representing spaces, hard spaces, tabs, centering, and indents.

SIZE

Choosing a Font Size

Keyboard

1. Move the insertion point where you want to begin formatting text.
2. Choose Layout, Font. (Or press F9.)
3. Select the Font Size that you want. The sizes that are available depend upon the font face that is selected.
4. Choose OK.
5. Type the text.
6. Choose Layout, Font, and choose a different font size.

Mouse

1. Move the insertion point where you want to begin formatting text.
2. Click on the Font Size button in the Power Bar.
3. Select the font size. The sizes that are available depend upon the font face that is selected.
4. Type text.
5. Click on the Font Size button and select a different font size.

Formats text in the font size that you want. An example of the results will be shown in the Font dialog box. Use these same steps to apply a different font size to a selected block of text (*see also* FONTS).

Choosing a Relative Size

Keyboard

1. Move the insertion point where you want to begin formatting text.
2. Choose Layout, Font. (Or press F9.)
3. Choose Relative Size and select the size from the pop-up list.

4. Choose OK.
5. Type the text.
6. Choose Layout, Font, Normal from the Relative Size list to return to the original font, or choose a different size.

Mouse

1. Move the insertion point where you want to begin formatting text.
2. Click the right mouse button and choose Font. Then follow the preceding steps 3 through 6.

Applies a new size to the text. You can also select a block of text and use these steps to apply a new size to it.

The choices of size are Fine, Small, Normal, Large, Very Large, and Extra Large. The example box in the Font dialog box shows an example of each when it is selected. The actual size depends upon the type of font face that is being used in the document. For example, if you are using Times Roman type face and you choose Fine, WordPerfect will probably select a 6- or 8-point font size. The font size adjustment is made automatically.

Note *You can choose File, Preferences, Print and change the percentage that controls the size of the font that is used when you select a relative size.*

SMALL CAPS

See CASE

SORT

Sorting Records

1. Select the text to be sorted; or if the entire document is to be sorted, you do not need to select it. For example, if

the document consists only of a list (no titles or headings) you can sort without selecting it.

2. Choose Tools, Sort. (Or press ALT+F9.)
3. Choose OK.

Sorts the first word in each line ending with a hard return in alphabetical ascending order.

You can specify other conditions for the sort. Choose any of the following to make changes.

- *Input File* chooses a file saved to disk and displays it in the document window.
- *Output File* saves the results of the sort in the file named here.
- The options in the Sort By box select the record type that corresponds to the text to be sorted:

  Line is text ending with one hard return.
  Paragraph is text ending with two or more hard returns.
  Merge Record is information in a merge data file.
  Table Row is available only when the insertion point is in a table.
  Column is available only when the insertion point is in column formatting.

Entering Key Definitions

1. Select the text to be sorted, or use the entire document.
2. Choose Tools, Sort. (Or press ALT+F9.)
3. Select the record type to Sort By.
4. Select Key 1 to be defined. A greater-than symbol (>) at the left of the key number indicates the selected key. See step 8 or 9 to add or insert keys.
5. Choose a type—Alpha or Numeric, depending on the information to be sorted.
6. Choose a sort order—Ascending or Descending.
7. Enter numbers in the text boxes to specify the Line, Field, Word, Columns, or Cells to be sorted. See the list

below for a description of each, depending on the record type that is selected to Sort By.

8. You can choose Add Key to add and define extra keys as needed. Nine keys can be defined. The sort will be on the basis of the first key, then the second key, and so on.
9. You can choose Insert Key to insert a new key above the key that is currently selected.
10. You can choose Delete Key to remove the selected key. Key 1 always has to be defined and cannot be deleted.
11. Choose OK when done.

Designates the fields, words, or lines that will determine the order in which information is sorted.

Defining keys is used to sort multiple information. For example, assume you wanted to sort last names, where each name is on a separate line, and the last name is the second word in the first field. Choose Line as the type of sort. Then in Key 1, enter **1** for the Field; enter **2** for the Word—or you can enter **-1** for the word to count from the right to left rather than from the left to right. You would do this to sort on the basis of the last word in the field if some names consisted of more than two words.

The following describes the entries in a key depending upon the record type that is selected to Sort By.

- Line type (each line ends with a hard return):
  Fields are separated by one tab.
  Words are separated by one space.

- Paragraph type (lines end with two or more hard returns):
  Fields are separated by one tab.
  Lines are text ending with a soft or hard return.
  Words are separated by one space.

- Merge records (information in a merge data file):
  Fields end with an ENDFIELD code.
  Lines end with a soft or hard return.
  Words are separated by one space.

- Parallel columns:
  Columns are separated by hard page breaks.
  Lines end with a soft or hard return.
  Words are separated by one space.

- Table:
  Cells are identified by a cell address.
  Lines end with soft or hard returns.
  Words are separated by one space.

Selecting Records

1. Select the text or use the entire document.
2. Choose Tools, Sort. (Or press ALT+F9.)
3. Select the record type to Sort By.
4. Define the keys. For example, if you want to select records on the basis of information that is in the fifth field, enter **5** in the Field text box to define Key 1. (You can define more than one key for selecting records just as you do for sorting.)
5. Choose Select Records. The status bar now shows operators.
6. Enter the record selection statement. (See examples in the following list.)
7. If you like, choose Select Without Sorting to not sort the output.
8. Choose OK.

Displays only selected records depending on the instructions in the record selection statement. If you want to restore other records that were in the document, click immediately on the Undo button or press CTRL+Z.

The keys must be defined to correspond to the select statement in the Record Selection text box. The following are examples of record statements that can be entered using the commands shown in the status bar when selecting records.

Command	Statement	Selection Result
| OR (or)	Key 1=Brown | Key 2=WA	All records containing the word "Brown", or "WA"
& AND (and)	Key 1=Brown & Key 2=WA	Only records containing both "Brown" and "WA"
= (equal)	Key 1=Los Angeles	Only records containing "Los Angeles"
<> (not equal)	Key 1<>WA	All records except those containing "WA"
> (greater than)	Key 1>98000	All records containing ZIP codes greater than 98000
< (less than)	Key 1<98000	All records containing ZIP codes less than 98000
>= (equal to or greater than)	Key 1>=98004	All records containing ZIP code 98004 or greater
=< (equal to or less than)	Key 1=<98004	All records containing ZIP code 98004 or less

SPACING

See LINE SPACING, PARAGRAPH SPACING, and WORD/LETTER SPACING

SPELLER

Keyboard

1. Choose Tools, Speller. (Or press CTRL+F1.)
2. Choose Start.

3. At the first misspelled word (or word that is not in the dictionary), a suggested correct spelling is displayed in the Replace With text box.
4. Choose Replace to correct the misspelled word. If you want to replace with a different word, select the word from the list of Suggestions; or choose Replace With to move the insertion point into the text box and type the correct spelling, and then choose Replace.
5. Repeat for additional words that are highlighted, or you can choose other options. (See the available options in the following list.)
6. Choose Yes at the end of the spell check to close it and return to the document.

Mouse

1. Click on the Speller button in the Power Bar. Then follow the preceding steps 2 through 6.

Checks the spelling of document words on the basis of comparison to words in the WordPerfect dictionary. Words that do not match are highlighted. You can then change them, or if they are spelled correctly, you can ignore and move to the next word that doesn't match.

Other options that can be selected during the spell check are

- *Add To* selects the dictionary to which you can add words that are not in the main dictionary.
- *Skip Once* makes no correction to a highlighted word and goes on. The spell checker will stop at the next occurrence of this same word.
- *Skip Always* makes no correction to a highlighted word and skips all remaining words spelled exactly like it.
- *Add* adds the highlighted word to the dictionary displayed in the Add To text box.
- *Suggest* shows additional words in the Suggestions list.

Choosing Items From the Speller Menu Bar

Keyboard

1. Choose Tools, Speller. (Or press CTRL+F1.)
2. Choose the items that you want. (See the following list for a description of the choices.)
3. Choose Close or run the spell check.

Mouse

1. Click on the Speller button in the Power Bar. Then follow the preceding steps 2 and 3.

Controls the way the speller checks for items in the document. You may want to turn off some options to speed up the spelling check.

The items are

- *Check* specifies the item to be checked. Document is the default, and the insertion point can be any place in the document. Other choices depend upon the position of the insertion point.
- *Dictionaries* designates the dictionary to be used during the spell check, either Main or Supplementary (*see* "Selecting Spelling Dictionaries").
- *Options* selects the items that you do or do not want to check. Exhaustive Checking, if allowed, looks for suggestions in languages not usually used in a spell check.

Note *The choices selected here can be made permanent (default) choices. To do this choose File, Preferences, Writing Tools, select WordPerfect Speller and choose Setup. Then make the changes in the Speller Setup dialog box.*

Selecting Spelling Dictionaries

Keyboard

1. Choose Tools, Speller. (Or press CTRL+F1.)
2. Choose Add To.

3. Choose the spelling dictionary that you want to add words to during the current spell check. (See a description of each type in the list below.)
4. Run the spell check and choose Add at the words you want to add to the dictionary.

Mouse

1. Click on the Speller button in the Power Bar. Then follow the preceding steps 2 through 4.

Designates the type of dictionary to which you can add words during the spell check. The dictionaries are

- *Document Dictionary* saves words with the current document. This dictionary is not available for use in checking the spelling in other documents. You may want to use this for a document that contains technical terms, foreign phrases, or unique text not generally used in other documents.
- *wpspelus.sup* contains words that are not in the main dictionary. If you choose to add words to the supplementary dictionary, they will be available in subsequent spell checks on other documents.

Editing Words in the Supplementary or Document Dictionaries

Keyboard

1. Choose Tools, Speller. (Or press CTRL+F1.)
2. Choose Dictionaries, Supplementary.
3. Choose either wpspelus.sup or Document Dictionary, or any other dictionary that you may have created that is listed.

   Note *Main Dictionary is the WordPerfect dictionary and cannot be accessed to edit words or to add words to.*

4. Choose Edit.
5. Select the words you want to change and either choose Delete to remove the word, or choose Edit. In the Edit Word Phrase dialog box, you can change the spelling or

edit the options for the word, including entering a replacement word or entering a list of alternative words.

6. Choose OK when done.
7. If you like, choose Add in the Edit dialog box to type new words and add them to the Supplementary Dictionary. Choose OK to leave the Add Word dialog box.
8. Choose Close to leave the Edit dialog box.
9. Choose Close to return to the Speller dialog box, and Close again to return to the document.

Mouse

1. Click on the Speller button in the Power Bar. Then follow the preceding steps 2 through 9.

Adds or edits words in the dictionaries other than the Main Dictionary. This allows you to enter names of individuals or places that are not in the Main Dictionary. With these names already contained in a dictionary, your spell check will be speeded up by not having to stop at them, unless they are not spelled the way they are entered in the Supplementary or Document Dictionary.

Note *You can also create a new Supplementary Dictionary. Choose Tools, Speller, Dictionaries, Supplementary, Create. Type a name for the dictionary in the Filename text box. Choose OK and Yes to create it. Then you can use the previous steps to enter words in the new dictionary.*

SPREADSHEET

See IMPORT DATA

STRIKEOUT

Keyboard

1. Move the insertion point to the place where you want to begin strikeout.

2. Choose Layout, Font. (Or press F9.)
3. Choose Strikeout.
4. Choose OK.
5. Type the text to be formatted with strikeout.
6. Choose Layout, Font, Strikeout to end, or press RIGHT ARROW to move the insertion point to the right of the end code. You may have to go to Reveal Codes for this.

Mouse

1. Move the insertion point to the place where you want to begin strikeout.
2. Click the right mouse button and choose Font. Then follow the preceding steps 3 through 6.

Formats text with the strikeout character. This is frequently used if you want to mark text for deletion, but keep it until a final decision is made to either leave it or remove it. You can also select a block of text and use these same steps to apply strikeout to the selection.

STYLES

Creating a Style

Keyboard

1. Choose Layout, Styles. (Or press ALT+F8.)
2. Choose Create.
3. Choose Style Name and type a name in the text box. For example, type **Title** for a style that is going to be used for a title.
4. Choose Description, if you like, and type a description in the text box. For example, type **Centered, TR 30 pts.** The description will appear in the Style List when the style is chosen.
5. Choose the Type of style—Paragraph (Paired), Character (Paired), or Document (Open). *Paired* includes a beginning and an ending code in the style similar to

beginning and ending codes for character formatting. *Open* contains only a beginning code similar to codes that are inserted for changing margins, tabs, or line spacing.

6. If you are creating a Paragraph type style, choose Enter Key will Chain to: and choose either <Same Style> to repeat the style when ENTER is pressed, or <None> to end the style formatting when ENTER is pressed.
7. Choose Contents and use the Styles Editor menu to insert codes for formatting, graphics, tables, commands, or other WordPerfect features. You can also enter text here. To insert a page code in the Contents box, press CTRL+SHIFT+ENTER. To insert a tab, press CTRL+TAB. To insert a hard space, press CTRL+SPACEBAR. To insert a hard return press SHIFT+ENTER.
8. Choose OK when done. The style name is added to the Style List.
9. Choose Close to return to the document.

Mouse

1. Click on the Styles button in the Button Bar. Then follow the preceding steps 2 through 9.

Creates a style consisting of formatting commands, graphics, text, or other features that are combined and can be applied to text in one step. Styles ensure consistency in formatting, which is especially useful in working with documents that contain multiple headings or other special formatting features.

Applying a Style

Keyboard

1. Move the insertion point to the place where you want to begin using the style, or select the text.
2. Choose Layout, Styles. (Or press ALT+F8.)
3. Select the style.
4. Choose Apply.

5. Type the text using the style, and end the formatting by choosing another style or by pressing ENTER if that applies to the selected style. Otherwise, skip this step if you are applying the style to selected text, or if the style does not require typing text (perhaps the style inserts a graphic or pretyped text).

Mouse

1. Move the insertion point to the place where you want to begin using the style, or select the text.
2. Click on the Styles button in the Button Bar.
3. Double-click on the style that you want to apply.

Formats text with the selected style, or inserts text, graphics, tables, or other WordPerfect features.

Editing a Style

Keyboard

1. Choose Layout, Styles. (Or press ALT+F8.)
2. Select the style.
3. Choose Edit.
4. Make changes in the Styles Editor using the same procedure that you used for creating a style.
5. Choose OK and Close to return to the document.

Mouse

1. Click on the Styles button in the Button Bar. Then follow the preceding steps 2 through 5.

Changes the characteristics of the selected style. When the change is made, it is applied automatically to all text in the document that is formatted with this style. This is a quick way of making formatting changes, particularly in a large document.

Saving Styles

Keyboard

1. Choose Layout, Styles. (Or press ALT+F8.)
2. Choose Options, Save As.

3. Do one of the following:

   - Type only a filename to save the styles in the TEMPLATE directory.
   - Type a path and filename to save it in a directory other than the TEMPLATE directory. For example, type **c:\wpwin\wpdocs*filename*** to save it in the WPDOCS directory.
     If you save the current document, the styles will be saved with the document.

4. Choose a Style Type. Both is the default; User Styles are created by the user and are not stored with system styles; System Styles are stored in the WordPerfect program files and affect headers, footers, outlining, and so on.
5. Choose OK and Close to return to the document.

Mouse

1. Click on the Styles button in the Button Bar. Then follow the preceding steps 2 through 5.

Saves the styles for use at a later time. By using the same set of styles with multiple documents, you can ensure consistency in formatting among them. For example, if you are creating several chapters of a book, with each chapter as a separate file, you can use the same set of styles in each document (*see* "Retrieving Styles," next, for information about this).

Retrieving Styles

Keyboard

1. Choose Layout, Styles. (Or press ALT+F8.)
2. Choose Options, Retrieve.
3. Enter the path and filename; or click on the button at the end of the text box, and choose from the Select File dialog box. Use one of the following:

   - If you saved the styles with a document, select that document and choose OK. Choose OK and Yes when asked to overwrite current styles, or No if you want to add the styles to the current list.

- If you saved the styles as a separate file, show the files in the TEMPLATE directory (double-click on WPWIN60 if necessary, then double-click on TEMPLATE). Select the file containing the styles you want and choose OK. Choose OK and Yes to overwrite current styles or choose No if you want to *add* the styles to the current list rather than replace.

4. Choose Close to return to the document.

Mouse

1. Click on the Styles button in the Button Bar. Then follow the preceding steps 2 through 4.

Opens the file containing the styles you want to use in the current document. Depending upon how the styles were saved, either a template will be chosen, or the styles will be copied from another document to the current document.

Using Other Options That Affect Styles

Keyboard

1. Choose Layout, Styles. (Or press ALT+F8.)
2. Choose Options and select the option that you want. (See the description of each in the following list.)
3. Choose Close to return to the document.

Mouse

1. Click on the Styles button in the Button Bar. Then follow the preceding steps 2 and 3.

Controls where styles are stored; also used to copy or delete individual styles.

The choices in the list of options are

- *Setup* turns on the choices you want displayed or specifies where you want the styles displayed. If you choose System Styles, they will be displayed in the Styles list and can be applied to the current document. Default Location indicates where the styles are stored. Current Document is the default choice.

- *Copy* copies a selected style from the current document to a template or to another document; or if you opened a template, you can copy a style from the template to a document or to another template.
- *Delete* removes a selected style from the list. You cannot delete system styles.
- *Reset* restores system styles that have been edited to their original settings.

Using QuickCreate

Keyboard

1. Move the insertion point to the position in the document where the codes are placed that you want to include in a style. For example, if you format a paragraph with various formatting codes, just move the insertion point to that paragraph.
2. Choose Layout, Styles. (Or press ALT+F8.)
3. Choose QuickCreate.
4. Type a name and a description for the style.
5. Choose Paragraph or Character to designate the style type.
6. Choose OK.

Mouse

1. Move the insertion point to the position in the document where the codes are placed that you want to include in a style. For example, if you format a paragraph with various formatting codes, just move the insertion point to that paragraph.
2. Click on the Styles button in the Button Bar. Then follow the preceding steps 3 through 6.

Creates a style from the current paragraph or character. The new style is added to the Style List. If you select the new style name and choose Edit, you will see the codes in the Styles Editor dialog box.

If you choose a Paragraph type, you can edit the style to designate how pressing ENTER chains to the next paragraph.

SUBDIVIDE

1. Choose Layout, Page.
2. Choose Subdivide Page.
3. Enter the number of columns or click on the arrows to select a number.
4. Enter the number of rows or click on the arrows to select a number.
5. Choose OK.
6. Enter text, graphics, and so on in each section.
7. Choose Layout, Page, Subdivide Page, Off to end subdividing. Subdivisions will fill the current page, even if they are empty, and the next physical page will be a full page without the subdivisions.

Divides the page into sections. Each section (subdivision) is referred to as a *logical* page. All sections are on a *physical* page (your actual paper size). The status bar shows the logical page number where the insertion point is located.

To move from one logical page to the next press ALT+PG DN; to go to the previous logical page, press ALT+PG UP. You can also use Edit, Go To and enter a page number to go to that logical page.

Use this feature to create programs, tickets, cards, booklets, or anything that you want to place on a full physical page. Headers, footers, page numbers, and so on can be included and will be printed on each logical page.

SUPERSCRIPT OR SUBSCRIPT

1. Move the insertion point to the place where you want to begin superscript or subscript, or select the text.
2. Choose Layout, Font. (Or press F9.)
3. Choose Position and choose Superscript or Subscript from the pop-up list.
4. Choose OK.
5. Type the character(s) to be formatted in superscript or subscript.
6. Choose Layout, Font. (Or press F9.)
7. Choose Position, Normal.
8. Choose OK.

Formats text characters in *superscript*, which moves the characters up above the baseline and reduces the size of the characters; or in *subscript*, which moves the characters below the baseline and reduces the size of the characters.

SUPPRESS

1. Move the insertion point to the page where you want to suppress some features.
2. Choose Layout, Page.
3. Choose Suppress.
4. Choose the items to suppress (be sure an X is displayed in the box) or choose All.
5. Choose OK.

Turns off selected features for the current page, but they will be printed again on the following pages. This is used, for example, if you have several sections of a document in one file and do not want to display headers or footers on the first page of each section.

Features that can be suppressed are headers, footers, watermarks, and page numbering. You can, however, choose Print Page Number at Bottom Center or Current Page so a page number will be shown regardless of other items that are turned off.

A delay code is inserted at the top of the page where the suppress code is located. To delay formatting or features for several pages at the beginning of the document, use the Delay Code feature (*see also* DELAY CODES).

TABLE OF AUTHORITIES

Designing the Table

A table of authorities lists citations for legal briefs and is similar to a table of contents; however, it can consist of more than one section. Each section contains a list of cases, or statutes, or regulations. Before marking the text for the table of authorities, determine the types of sections that you want. They frequently are any of the following: Cases, Statutory Provisions, Regulatory Provisions, and Constitutional Provisions.

Marking Text

Use the following steps to enter full form and short form marks for all authorities to be included in one section. Then repeat entering full form and short form marks for the next section, and so on.

Entering Full Form Marks

1. Choose Tools, Table of Authorities. A feature bar is displayed.
2. Select the first occurrence of the authority (such as a specific case).
3. Choose Create Full Form.
4. Type a name in the Section Name text box.

5. The selected text appears in the Short Form text box; however, it can be changed—perhaps shortened—if you like. This name is used only to mark other occurrences of the same authority, such as a specific case that is referred to several times in the document.
6. Choose OK to go to the window where you can edit the text.
7. Edit the full form text as you want it to appear in the table of authorities. For example, full form text for a case could be "Jones v. Washington, 555 U.S. 222 (1993)."
8. Choose Close to return to the document window. The table of authorities feature bar remains in the window.

Creates the full form reference name, which will appear in the table of authorities and which also marks the first occurrence of the authority.

Entering Short Form Marks

1. Select the next occurrence of the same authority that you just marked for a full form (for example, a reference to the same case). If you like, use Edit, Find to locate it.
2. If you need to display the feature bar again, choose Tools, Table of Authorities.
3. If you entered a short form name when you entered the full form mark, the name will appear in the Short Form text box. If the name is not displayed, type the short form name or select it from the list.
4. Choose Mark.
5. Repeat steps 1, 3, and 4 for additional occurrences of the same authority.

Creates a short name (form) to be used in place of the full form to mark subsequent occurrences of the same authority.

Defining and Generating the Table

1. Type an appropriate heading at the position where you want to enter the list for the first section and insert two or three blank lines. This can be on a new page at the end of the document.

2. If you need to display the feature bar, choose Tools, Table of Authorities.
3. Choose Define.
4. Select the definition from the list of Section Names.
5. Choose Edit. If you want to change the numbering Position, select it and choose a new position from the list.
6. If you want to change the Page Numbering style, select it and choose the format. Choose OK to leave the Page Number Format dialog box.
7. Choose OK to leave the Edit Table of Authorities box.
8. Choose Insert to insert the definition code. (Be sure the Section Name is selected.)
9. Repeat steps 1 through 8 for additional sections.
10. Choose Generate and OK.

Displays a list of authorities and corresponding page numbers in each appropriate section.

TABLE OF CONTENTS

Marking Text

1. Select the text to appear in the table of contents (heading, titles, and so on).
2. Choose Tools, Table of Contents.
3. Choose the Mark # (the level number is displayed for each level) for the appropriate heading level.
4. Repeat steps 1 through 3 for all additional entries.

Marks the text that you want to be included in the table of contents. This text can be edited in the table of contents later, if you like. You may want to change the case or other formatting.

Defining and Generating the Table of Contents

1. Move the insertion point to the page where you want to insert the table of contents. If you want it to be at the beginning of the document, press CTRL+ENTER at the top of the document, then move the insertion point up to the top of the new first page.
2. Type an appropriate heading or title for the table of contents and insert two or three blank lines.
3. If you need to display the feature bar, choose Tools, Table of Contents.
4. Choose Define.
5. Choose the Number of Levels (1-5) either by typing the number or clicking on the arrows to select the number.
6. If you like, choose Position for each level and select a page number position. Also choose Page Numbering to select a type of page number. If you want to use volume numbers, chapter numbers, and so on, choose Insert in the Page Number Format dialog box and then choose OK to return to the Define Table of Contents dialog box.
7. If you want the last level to be flush left rather than indented, turn on Display Last Level in Wrapped Format.
8. Choose OK. Be sure the definition code is inserted in the document.
9. Choose Generate and OK.

Inserts a table of contents at the definition code. The table of contents contains the text that is marked in the document and the corresponding page numbers, if you choose to include them.

If text is added and page numbers for the various items change as a result, mark any additional text that you want to include in the table of contents and choose Tools, Table of Contents. Then generate again without changing the definition.

Note *You can also choose Styles in the Define Table of Contents dialog box to apply a style type to each level in the table of contents. These styles can be edited the same way you edit any other type of style.* See also *STYLES.*

TABLES

Creating a Table

Keyboard

1. Move the insertion point to the place where you want to insert a table.
2. Choose Table, Create. (Or press F12.)
3. Choose Table if it is not already turned on.
4. Enter the number of Columns or select from the list.
5. Enter the number of Rows or select from the list.
6. Choose OK.

Mouse

1. Move the insertion point to the place where you want to insert a table.
2. Point to the Table Quick Create button in the Power Bar, and drag in the example table to select the number of columns and rows you want. The example expands as needed as you drag down or to the right.

Displays a table consisting of columns and rows at the insertion point.

Note *At step 3 in the Keyboard instructions, the other choice in the Create Table dialog box is Floating Cell. A floating cell is a paired code (beginning and ending codes) placed in document text (not in a table) and is used to refer to data in a table, column, row, cell, or other floating cells.*

Entering Information in the Table

1. Type the information in cell A1. Cell addresses are now displayed in the status bar.

2. Press TAB to go to cell B1 and type.
3. Repeat to go to the next cell or row.

Enters text or other information in cells. Cell addresses are displayed in the status bar along with the name of the table—Table A, Table B, and so on. If TAB is pressed in the last cell in the table (lower-right corner), an additional row is added.

You can click on any cell to move to it and edit, just as you do in regular document text.

Note *To insert a tab within a cell, press CTRL+TAB.*

Formatting Choices

Keyboard

1. Move the insertion point to the table.
2. Choose Table, Format. (Or press CTRL+F12.)
3. Choose any of the following, depending on what you are formatting:

   - *Cell* formats the cell where the insertion point is located and includes selecting Vertical Alignment, setting Justification similar to regular document text, and applying appearance and font attributes, or turning on Use Column Appearance and Text Size.
   - *Column* formats the column where the insertion point is located and includes setting Justification, selecting the number of digits after a decimal, setting margins within columns, and setting column width. You can also apply appearance and font attributes to the text in the entire column similar to using the Layout, Font dialog box.
   - *Row* formats the row where the insertion point is located and includes setting the number of lines per row, controlling row height—either automatic or fixed—setting top or bottom margins, and designating the row as a Header row that will be repeated at the top of each following page.

- *Table* formats the entire table and includes applying appearance and font attributes; setting justification, digits after decimals, and position from the right; setting left or right margins in columns; and setting column widths. You also can select a Table Position in relation to the page—Left, Right, Center, Full, or From Left Edge (enter a measurement for the distance from the left edge).

4. Choose OK to return to the table.

Mouse

1. Move the insertion point into the table.
2. Hold down the right mouse button and select Format. Then follow the preceding steps 3 and 4.

Changes the size and appearance of the entire table or of specific cells, columns, or rows, and formats information within the table.

Note *To quickly increase the width of a column, move the insertion point to any cell in the column, and press CTRL+.. To decrease the width of a column, press CTRL+,.*

Using Other Table Options

1. Move the insertion point to the table.
2. Choose Table.
3. Choose any of the other options in the table menu that you want to change. A description of each is shown in the list below. (The options affecting calculations and formulas are discussed later in this section.)
4. Choose OK to return to the table.

Changes other characteristics of the table in addition to the formatting changes discussed previously. The options are

- *Number type* (press ALT+F12) selects Accounting, Commas, Currency, Date/Time, and so on for Cell, Columns, or entire table.
- *Lines/Fill* (press SHIFT+F12) selects styles and fill options. Click on the button for each line to see

examples of the line styles and select one; or click on the arrow for each line to see the list of style names and select one. You can also set colors and fill options here. If you choose Table in this dialog box, you can change the default settings for the line style—select the line style you want, choose Use as Default and choose OK.

- *Insert* inserts additional rows or columns. Specify whether to insert before or after the insertion point.
- *Delete* removes columns, rows, or cell contents.
- *Join* combines cells or tables. Select the cells or tables first and then choose Table, Join.
- *Split* splits the cell or table. If you choose to split a table, the insertion point cannot be in the first row.
- *Names* changes the names of tables that are displayed in the status bar. Choose Create to create a new name.

Moving Around in a Table

Keyboard

Movement	Keypress
One cell to the right	TAB
One cell to the left	SHIFT+TAB
Up one cell	UP ARROW
Down one cell	DOWN ARROW
First cell in row	HOME, HOME
Last cell in row	END, END
Top line in cell	ALT+HOME
Last line in cell	ALT+END

Mouse

1. Click on any cell to move to it.

Moves the insertion point to a position in the table where you can enter or edit information.

Calculating a Total of Values in a Table

1. Move the insertion point to the cell where you want to display the sum.
2. Choose Table, Sum. (Or press CTRL+=.)

Totals the numbers in the row or column and displays the sum in the cell where the insertion point is located.

Inserting a Math Formula in a Table

1. Choose Table. Be sure Cell Formula Entry is checked. If it is not turned on, you cannot enter formulas in cells.
2. Choose Table, Formula Bar.
3. Move the insertion point to the cell where you want to place the formula.
4. Enter the formula in the Edit Formula text box at the top of the feature bar. For example, if you want to multiply the value in A1 by the value in B1 and place the results in C1 (where the insertion point is in step 3), type **A1*B1**
5. Click on the Insert button (shows a check mark). The result of the calculation will be inserted in the cell.

Calculates the values in cells as designated by the formula that is entered in the cells. If the values that are calculated are changed, move the insertion point to the cell containing the formula results and choose Calculate. The value will be updated.

Choose Functions to choose math functions that can be inserted in the formula. Select the function and choose Insert.

Copying a Formula

1. Move the insertion point to the cell containing the formula to be copied.
2. Choose Table, Copy Formula; or choose Copy Formula from the feature bar if it is displayed.
3. Enter the cell name that is the destination cell; or choose Down and select the number of cells to copy to; or choose Right and select the number of cells to copy to.

4. Choose OK.

Copies an existing formula from one cell to another cell, or copies the formula down or to the right a specified number of cells and displays the results of the calculation in those cells.

TABS

See also RULER BAR

Setting Tabs

Keyboard

1. Move the insertion point to the line where you want to change the tab settings.
2. Choose Layout, Line.
3. Choose Tab Set.
4. Choose Clear All to remove the existing tabs.
5. Choose Type and select the type of tab from the pop-up list. (See a description of the types of tabs in the following list.)
6. Choose Position and enter the measurement, or click on the arrows and select a measurement.
7. If you like, choose Repeat Every and enter a measurement. This will set tabs at intervals of equal length across the line.
8. Choose Set.
9. If you did not turn on Repeat Every, use steps 5, 6, and 8 to set additional tabs.
10. Choose Left Margin (Relative) or Left Edge of Paper (Absolute). *Left Margin (Relative)* means if the left margin is changed, the positions of the tabs will move to the left or right depending on the margin change. *Left Edge of Paper (Absolute)* means the tab sets will remain at the same position regardless of any change to the left margin.
11. Choose OK.

Mouse

1. Move the insertion point to the line where you want to change the tab settings.
2. Drag on the Tab Set button in the Power Bar and choose Set Tabs, or press ALT+SHIFT+F3 to display the ruler bar at the top of the document window.
3. Drag on the Tab Set button and choose Clear All Tabs.
4. Drag on the Tab Set button again and choose the type of tab setting. (See a description of the types of tabs in the following list.) The default is a Left tab. The button displays the letter indicating the type of tab.
5. Click on the position(s) in the ruler (click on the space below the numbers) where you want to set the tab(s).
6. If needed, repeat steps 4 and 5 to set other types of tabs.

Inserts new tab settings that are in effect from the insertion point on in the active document. A tab set code [Tab Set] is displayed in Reveal Codes to indicate where the new tabs begin.

Tab types are

- *Left* aligns the left side of the text at the tab setting.
- *Center* centers text on either side of the tab setting.
- *Right* aligns the right side of the text at the tab setting.
- *Decimal* aligns decimals in numbers (or text) at the tab setting.
- *Dot Left, Dot Center, Dot Right,* or *Dot Decimal* sets a tab with dot leaders. A tab with dot leaders inserts dots between the tab and the previous tab setting. Each type of tab can be set with a dot leader.

You can change the leader character in the Tab Set dialog box. Just type a different character in the Dot Leader Character box. Also, specify Spaces Between Characters if you want to change that from 1.

The default align character for decimal tabs is a period. That can be changed to a comma or any other appropriate character. Choose Character, located beneath Align Character, and type the alignment character that you want.

Note *To use the tabs, press the TAB key to move to the first tab, type text, press TAB to move to the next tab, type text, and so on.*

Restoring Default Tabs

1. Move the insertion point to the line where you want to restore the default tab settings.
2. Choose Layout, Line.
3. Choose Tab Set.
4. Choose Default.
5. Choose OK.

Inserts the default tabs at the insertion point. The default tabs are Left tabs set every 1/2 inch, and the default, which is Position From, is Left Margin, (Relative).

TEMPLATE

Choosing a Supplied Template

1. Choose File, Template. (Or press CTRL+T.)
2. Select the template you want. A description is shown in the Description box located below the list of document template names.
3. If you like, choose View to see the contents of the template.
4. Choose OK.

Opens the selected template. A template can contain formatting commands, boilerplate text, tables, graphics, macros, styles, or other program options used to create a specific type of document.

The Standard template is the default used with all documents, unless you choose one of the other predefined templates. When you use a predefined template, any changes to the template are only saved with the document. When you use the template with another document, it has its original text, formatting, styles, and so on.

Creating a Template

1. Choose File, Template. (Or press CTRL+T.)
2. Choose Options.
3. Choose Create Template.
4. Type a name for the new template in the Name text box.
5. If you like, choose Name in the Template to Base On box, and click on the arrows to display a list of available templates, and choose the one you want.
6. Choose OK. A feature bar is displayed and you can choose the following:

   - *Create Object* inserts Styles, Macro, Abbreviations, Button Bar, Keyboard, or Menu in the template. Work with these features the same way you work with them in a document.
   - *Copy/Remove Object* copies an object type from another template. The text boxes at the bottom of the dialog box show corresponding lists of items. Select the items you want to copy or remove, and then choose Copy, Remove, Copy All, or Remove All.
   - *Associate* associates a template object with a WordPerfect feature (if there is an association) whenever the template is used. Or choose Triggers to play a selected macro at a designated time—choose the time from the list box.
   - *Description* displays the description in the Template dialog box when a template is selected.
   - *Initial Style* creates a Document Initial Style for the template.
7. Enter any text, tables, and graphics in the document window.
8. Choose Exit Template, Yes when done to save the template.

Templates can store styles, macros, abbreviations, Button Bars, menus, and keyboard layout. You can also insert tables with formulas, watermarks, and graphics as well as text. Templates can be used in multiple documents, and are convenient when you frequently create documents that require special formatting such as registration or enrollment forms, reports, surveys, brochures, and newsletters. The formatting is saved and does not have to be repeated. Not only is this efficient, but it also ensures consistency among documents.

Editing a Template

1. Choose File, Template. (Or press CTRL+T.)
2. Select the template.
3. Choose Options, Edit Template.
4. Use the same procedures to make changes that you used to create the template.
5. Choose Exit Template, Yes when done to save the changes.

Changes contents and features in the template. You can also choose Delete Template from the Options menu in the template dialog box to remove a selected template from the directory.

TEXTART

Creating a TextArt Object

Keyboard

1. Move the insertion point to the place where you want to insert a TextArt object.
2. Choose Graphics, TextArt to go to the TextArt window. The insertion point is in the Enter Text box.
3. Enter the characters for the text art. (When you start entering characters, the selected text will be deleted.)
4. Select a shape for the text. To do this, press TAB enough times to move to the shapes box; press the arrow keys to

go to the shape you want (an outline is around each shape when you move to it); and press the SPACEBAR to select it (the button will be depressed.) The text is automatically displayed in the selected shape.

5. When done, choose File, Exit & Return to WordPerfect.
6. Choose Yes to update objects in WordPerfect and return to the document.

Mouse

1. Move the insertion point to the place where you want to insert a TextArt object.
2. Click on the TextArt button in the Button Bar to go to the TextArt window. The insertion point is in the Enter Text box.
3. Enter the characters for the text art. (When you start entering characters, the selected text will be deleted.)
4. Click on the shape that you want. The text is automatically displayed in the selected shape.
5. When done, double-click on the Control-menu box at the left end of the title bar.
6. Choose Yes to update object and return to the document window.

Displays text or other characters in the shape that is selected in the TextArt window. You can use this feature to produce logos, ads, watermarks, or any other graphics object.

Other options that can be used to change the display of the text art are available in the TextArt window. When an option is selected, instructions for using it are displayed in the status bar.

You can press CTRL+P in the TextArt window and print the text as it is displayed there. This is helpful, before returning to the document, to see exactly how the text will look when it is printed.

Editing a TextArt Object

Keyboard

1. Choose Graphics, Edit Box. (Or press SHIFT+F11.)
2. Select the box number. If the TextArt object is the only graphic in the document, it will be selected automatically.
3. Choose Edit, Edit TextArt Object.
4. Make changes using the same steps used for creating text art.
5. Choose File, Exit & Return to WordPerfect.
6. Choose Yes to return to the document window.

Mouse

1. Double-click on the TextArt object shown in the document window.
2. Make changes using the same steps used for creating text art.
3. Double-click on the Control-menu box at the left end of the title bar.
4. Choose Yes to update object and return to the document window.

Revises the text art graphic object.

THESAURUS

Keyboard

1. Move the insertion point to the word that you want to find a synonym or antonym for.
2. Choose Tools, Thesaurus. (Or press ALT+F1.)
3. Scroll through the list of words in the dialog box. Synonyms are shown first, then antonyms.

4. Select a new word for the word in the document. The selected word appears in the Word text box.
5. Choose Replace to replace the word in the document with a different word.

Mouse

1. Move the insertion point to the word that you want to find a synonym or antonym for.
2. Click on the Thesaurus button in the Power Bar. Then follow the preceding steps 3 through 5.

Displays words that have the same or similar meanings as the word in the document; or that have opposite meanings. In addition to replacing a word, you can also choose Look Up to display other words. In the box at the top of the list, the usage is indicated by a letter in parentheses.

Additional choices that can be made in the Thesaurus dialog box are

- *Dictionary* changes dictionaries. The choices here depend on the dictionaries that have been installed. To select the dictionary, choose Change Dictionary and select the dictionary from the list of filenames in the Select a WordPerfect Thesaurus dialog box.
- *Edit* uses Cut or Copy to move the word in the Word text box to the Clipboard. You can then paste it in the current document. Select All and Undo are also options here.
- *History* displays a list of words that you have looked up previously. You can select the word and see the list of synonyms and antonyms for that word again.

TYPEOVER

See the "Basics" section at the beginning of the book.

TYPESETTING

See ADVANCE, OVERSTRIKE, WORD/LETTER SPACING, and KERNING

UNDELETE

1. Move the insertion point to the place where you want to restore a previous deletion (any one of the last three).
2. Choose Edit, Undelete. (Or press CTRL+SHIFT+Z.) The last deletion is displayed as selected text at the insertion point.
3. Choose Restore to insert the deletion and remove the highlighting, or choose Next or Previous to see the other deletions. You can cycle through the three deletions to see them. When you display the one you want, choose Restore.

Restores a previous deletion at the insertion point. WordPerfect stores your last three deletions. Each deletion can be any size—a word, paragraph, page, or any amount of selected text.

UNDERLINE

Keyboard

1. Move the insertion point to the place where you want to begin underlining.
2. Choose Layout, Font, Underline. (Or press CTRL+U.)
3. Choose OK to return to the document. (Skip this step if you pressed CTRL+U.)
4. Type the text with underlining.
5. Choose Layout, Font, Underline and OK or press CTRL+U to end, or press the RIGHT ARROW key to move

to the right side of the end code. You may have to go to Reveal Codes to do this.

Mouse

1. Move the insertion point to the place where you want to begin underlining.
2. Click on the Underline Font button in the Power Bar.
3. Type the text with underlining.
4. Click on the Underline Font button to end the formatting.

Formats text with an underline. You can also select a block of text and apply underlining to it using any of these procedures.

UNDO

Keyboard

1. Leave the insertion point at the place where you want to reverse the last edit.
2. Choose Edit, Undo. (Or press CTRL+Z.)

Mouse

1. Leave the insertion point at the place where you want to reverse the last edit.
2. Click on the Undo button in the Power Bar.

Reverses the last edit, including deletions, added text, and so on.

UNITS OF MEASURE

1. Choose File, Preferences.
2. Choose Display.
3. Choose Units of Measure and select the type of measurement you want. The default is to display

measurements in inches followed by a quotation mark ("). Other choices are Inches followed by a lowercase *i*; Centimeters (c); Millimeters (m); Points (p); or 1200ths of an inch (w).

4. If you like, change the Status Bar/Ruler Display to correspond to the Units of Measure selection.
5. Choose OK.
6. Choose Close.

Changes, permanently, the units of measure displayed in any dialog box that contains a feature that requires a measurement, such as tabs, line height, and margins.

WATERMARK

Creating a Watermark

1. Choose Layout, Watermark.
2. Select either Watermark A or B. You can create two watermarks in a document.
3. Choose Create. A feature bar is displayed.
4. If you want to insert a WordPerfect figure or a file, choose Figure or File.
5. Select the filename for the figure or file that you want to use as a watermark, and choose OK to insert it.
6. You also can type text, or use any of the buttons in the Power Bar or Button Bar to insert tables, columns, or graphics for the watermark.
7. Choose Placement and designate the pages where you want the watermark to be inserted. Choose OK.
8. If you like, choose Next or Previous to see other watermarks in the current document.
9. Choose Close when done.

Places a watermark in the current document at the specified pages. Watermarks are in the background, and you can type text or place graphics or tables over them.

You can also use the WordPerfect menu to work with the objects or text that you are entering as watermarks. This includes going to the WordPerfect Draw window to create your own watermark, or inserting a WordPerfect Chart from the Chart window.

Choose Layout, Watermark, Discontinue to discontinue displaying on the next and following pages. If you want the watermark to be suppressed on one page, choose Layout, Page, Suppress; or insert a Delay Code to specify where to start showing the watermark.

Editing a Watermark

1. Move the insertion point to the page showing the watermark.
2. Choose Layout, Watermark.
3. Choose the watermark to be edited: Watermark A or B.
4. Choose Edit. Make any changes to text.
5. If you inserted a figure and want to edit it, choose Graphics, Edit box. Edit the graphic the same way you do for any other graphic image.
6. Choose Close enough times to remove the feature bars.

Edits the watermark image. For example, you can rotate the image or make changes the same way you edit other graphics.

Removing a Watermark

Keyboard

1. Choose View, Reveal Codes. (Or press ALT+F3.)
2. Select the watermark code.
3. Press DEL.

Mouse

1. Drag on the horizontal bars in the vertical scroll bar to display the Reveal Codes window.
2. Drag the watermark code from the Reveal Codes window.

Deletes the watermark from the active document.

WIDOW/ORPHAN

1. Move the insertion point to the place where you want to begin widow/orphan control.
2. Choose Layout, Page.
3. Choose Keep Text Together.
4. Choose Prevent the first and last lines of paragraphs from being separated across pages.
5. Choose OK.

Keeps the *first* or the *last* line of a paragraph together with other lines in the paragraph. A page break cannot separate these lines. Text will be squeezed on the first page, or bumped to the second page, depending on space available.

WORD COUNT

1. Choose File, Document Info.
2. After viewing the information, choose OK to remove the box from the window.

Displays the Document Information box containing information about the document. Included are number of words in the document, plus number of characters, lines, sentences, paragraphs, and pages. Also displayed are average word length, average words per sentence, and maximum words per sentence.

WORD/LETTER SPACING

1. Move the insertion point to the place where you want to adjust the spacing.

2. Choose Layout, Typesetting.
3. Choose Word/Letterspacing.
4. Make the spacing changes that you want. (See the following list for a description of the choices.)
5. Choose OK when done.

Adjusts word or letter spacing manually from the insertion point on. These changes can also be applied to selected text. This is frequently used to adjust the spacing in headlines, titles, and document headings, where you want to emphasize a portion of text.

- *Word Spacing* adjusts spacing between words. Choices are
  - *Normal* The spacing recommended by the font manual.
  - *WordPerfect Optimal* Spacing recommended by WordPerfect.
  - *Percent of Optimal* Spacing you can set manually. Enter a specification value.
- *Word Spacing Justification Limits* adjusts the amount of space between words when full justification is turned on. Choices are
  - *Compressed to:* The default is 60 percent.
  - *Expanded to:* The default is 400 percent.
- *Letterspacing* adjusts spacing between letters. Choices are the same as for "Word Spacing."

- *Line Height (Leading) Adjustment* adjusts spacing between lines. Turn on Adjust Leading and set a specific measurement for the space between lines, or choose from the list.

- *Automatic Kerning* can be turned on or off. When it's on, spacing adjusts automatically between some letters. The spacing is based on the font that is being used.

- *Baseline Placement* can be turned on or off (*see* BASELINE PLACEMENT).

WORDPERFECT CHARACTERS

See CHARACTERS

ZOOM

Showing the Entire Page

Keyboard

1. Move the insertion point to the page that you want to see.
2. Choose View, Zoom.
3. Choose Full Page.
4. Choose OK.

Mouse

1. Move the insertion point to the page that you want to see.
2. Click on the Page Zoom Full button in the Power Bar.

Displays a full page on the screen. Use this to see the position of page numbers, headers, and footers, and how the entire page will look when printed.

Returning to Regular Document Size

Keyboard

1. Choose View, Zoom.
2. Choose 100%.
3. Choose OK.

Mouse

1. Click on the Page Zoom Full button in the Power Bar.

Restores the document to the normal Page view.

Other Choices of Sizes

Keyboard

1. Move the insertion point to the page you want to view.
2. Choose View, Zoom.
3. Choose the size you want.
4. Choose OK.

Mouse

1. Move the insertion point to the page you want to view.
2. Click on the Zoom button in the Power Bar. (It shows 100% as the default.)
3. Drag to the size you want and release the mouse button.

Changes the document view to a specific size—100 percent is the normal document display. Choose amounts below 100 percent to reduce the size of the print, but to show more of the page. (Full page is 38 percent of the size of the normal document display.) Choose amounts over 100 percent to increase the size of the print, but to reduce the amount of page that you see. Choose Margin Width to display lines of text from the left side of the window to the right side. Choose Page Width to display the left and right edges of the page including the amount of margins. Choose Other to specify a percent under 50 percent or over 200 percent, as well as any percents not displayed in the list.

Appendix

Shortcut Keys

Feature or Command	Shortcut Key
Abbreviation, Expand	CTRL+A
Bold	CTRL+B
Bullets & Numbers (insert)	CTRL+SHIFT+B
Calculate document (in table)	ALT+SHIFT+F12
Case Toggle	CTRL+K
Center Justification	CTRL+E
Center a Line	SHIFT+F7
Character	CTRL+W
Close	CTRL+F4
Close Without Saving	CTRL+SHIFT+F4
Column, Decrease	CTRL+, (comma) or CTRL+SHIFT+,
Column, Increase	CTRL+. (period) or CTRL+SHIFT+.
Copy	CTRL+C
Cut	CTRL+X
Data Fill (in tables)	CTRL+SHIFT+F12
Date Code	CTRL+SHIFT+D
Date Text	CTRL+D
Decimal Tab	ALT+SHIFT+F7
Double Indent	CTRL+SHIFT+F7
Draft View	CTRL+F5
Edit Box	SHIFT+F11
Exit	ALT+F4
Feature Bar Pop-down Menu	ALT+SHIFT+F10
Figure (insert image)	F11
Find	F2
Find Next	SHIFT+F2

Feature or Command	Shortcut Key
Find Previous	ALT+F2
Flush Right (line)	ALT+F7
Font Dialog Box	CTRL+F or F9
Full Justification	CTRL+J
Generate	CTRL+F9
Go To	CTRL+G
Grammatik	ALT+SHIFT+F1
Hanging Indent	CTRL+F7
Hard Space	CTRL+SPACEBAR
Help Context	F1
Hide Bars	ALT+SHIFT+F5
Horizontal Line	CTRL+F11
Hyphen Character	CTRL+-
Hyphen, Soft	CTRL+SHIFT+-
Hyphenation Ignore	CTRL+/
Indent	F7
Italic	CTRL+I
Left Justification	CTRL+L
Lines/Fill (in tables)	SHIFT+F12
Macro, Play	ALT+F10
Macro, Record	CTRL+F10
Margin Release	SHIFT+TAB
Margins	CTRL+F8
Merge	SHIFT+F9
Move Cell Down	DOWN ARROW
Move Cell Up	UP ARROW
Move Char Next	RIGHT ARROW
Move Char Previous	LEFT ARROW
Move Column Next	ALT+RIGHT ARROW
Move Column or Page Bottom	ALT+END
Move Column or Page Top	ALT+HOME

Feature or Command	Shortcut Key
Move Column Previous	ALT+LEFT ARROW
Move Document Bottom	CTRL+END
Move Document Top	CTRL+HOME
Move Line Beginning	HOME
Move Line Down	DOWN ARROW
Move Line End	END
Move Line Up	UP ARROW
Move Page Next	ALT+PGDN
Move Page Previous	ALT+PGUP
Move Paragraph Next	CTRL+DOWN ARROW
Move Paragraph Previous	CTRL+UP ARROW
Move Screen Down	PGDN
Move Screen Up	PGUP
Move Word Next	CTRL+RIGHT ARROW
Move Word Previous	CTRL+LEFT ARROW
New Document	CTRL+N or SHIFT+F4
Next Open Document	CTRL+F6
Number Type (in tables)	ALT+F12
Open	CTRL+O or F4
Outline Body text (toggle)	CTRL+H or ALT+SHIFT+T
Outline Define	CTRL+SHIFT+O
Page Break	CTRL+ENTER
Page Number Display	CTRL+SHIFT+P
Page View	ALT+F5
Paste	CTRL+V
Previous Open Document	CTRL+SHIFT+F6
Print (dialog box)	F5
Print Document	CTRL+P
QuickMark Find	CTRL+Q
QuickMark Set	CTRL+SHIFT+Q
Redisplay (equation)	CTRL+F3

Feature or Command	Shortcut Key
Repeat	SHIFT+F10
Replace	CTRL+F2
Reveal Codes	ALT+F3
Right Justification	CTRL+R
Ruler Bar	ALT+SHIFT+F3
Save	CTRL+S or SHIFT+F3
Save All	CTRL+SHIFT+S
Save As	F3
Scroll Screen Left	CTRL+PGUP
Scroll Screen Right	CTRL+PGDN
Select (toggle on/off)	F8
Select Cell	SHIFT+F8
Select Cell Down	ALT+SHIFT+DOWN ARROW
Select Cell Up	ALT+SHIFT+UP ARROW
Select Char Next	SHIFT+RIGHT ARROW
Select Char Previous	SHIFT+LEFT ARROW
Select Column Bottom	ALT+SHIFT+END
Select Column Next	ALT+SHIFT+RIGHT ARROW
Select Column Previous	ALT+SHIFT+LEFT ARROW
Select Column Top	ALT+SHIFT+HOME
Select Document Bottom	CTRL+SHIFT+END
Select Document Top	CTRL+SHIFT+HOME
Select Line Beginning	SHIFT+HOME
Select Line Down	SHIFT+DOWN ARROW
Select Line End	SHIFT+END
Select Line Up	SHIFT+UP ARROW
Select Page Next	ALT+SHIFT+PGDN
Select Page Previous	ALT+SHIFT+PGUP
Select Paragraph Next	CTRL+SHIFT+DOWN ARROW
Select Paragraph Previous	CTRL+SHIFT+UP ARROW
Select Screen Down	SHIFT+PGDN

Feature or Command	Shortcut Key
Select Screen Up	SHIFT+PGUP
Select Word Next	CTRL+SHIFT+RIGHT ARROW
Select Word Previous	CTRL+SHIFT+LEFT ARROW
Show ¶ toggle	CTRL+SHIFT+F3
Sort	ALT+F9
Speller	CTRL+F1
Styles	ALT+F8
Sum (in table)	CTRL+=
Table, Create	F12
Table, Format	CTRL+F12
Template	CTRL+T
Text Box	ALT+F11
Thesaurus	ALT+F1
Undelete	CTRL+SHIFT+Z
Underline	CTRL+U
Undo	CTRL+Z
Vertical Line	CTRL+SHIFT+F11
What Is	SHIFT+F1
Window Next	ALT+F6
Window Previous	ALT+SHIFT+F6
Zoom Full Page	SHIFT+F5